Untethered Aging

Also by
William Keiper

Life Expectancy: It's Never Too Late to Change Your Game

The Power of Urgency: Playing to Win with Proactive Urgency

Cyber Crisis: It's Personal Now (also available as an audiobook)

Amazon for President

Apple for President

Walmart for President

Untethered Aging

William Keiper

FirstGlobal® Partners LLC

Steve Chandler, Editor and Foreword
Brannan Sirratt, Editorial Contributor
David Moratto, Cover and Interior Design—Print
Chris X. Nelson, eBook Design and Layout
Pixelparticle.com, Cover Photograph (via Shutterstock)
Chelsea J. Donoho, Author Photograph

The material provided herein is for general information and educational
purposes only. The publisher and author use reasonable efforts to include
accurate and up-to-date information; however, we make no warranties or
representations of accuracy, currency, or completeness.

Because of the internet's dynamic nature, any Web addresses in this book
may have changed since publication and may no longer be valid. The Covid-19
course and consequences are not fully known as of the date of publication.
References made to Covid-19 are as of the dates and from the sources
noted in the references and footnotes.

The publisher and author do not render psychiatric or psychological,
medical, legal, or other advice requiring licensure or certification.
The information contained herein may not apply to all situations
and may not reflect the most current situation.

Rather than use a trademark symbol with every usage of a trademarked
name, such names are used only in an editorial fashion and to the trademark
owner's benefit, with no intention of infringement, confusion, or ambiguity
as to ownership. All marks and tradenames are the property of their
respective companies.

Publisher contact: publisher@firstglobalpartners.com

Library of Congress Control Number: 2021902002
ISBN-13: 978-0-578-85503-5

For Alex Cyrell, Jeff Holtmeier,
Tom Liguori, and J. Thomas Long,
each a true friend and fellow warrior,
with gratitude.

"Do not let your fire go out, spark by irreplaceable spark in the hopeless swamps of the not-quite, the not-yet, and the not-at-all. Do not let the hero in your soul perish in lonely frustration for the life you deserved and have never been able to reach.
The world you desire can be won.
It exists... it is real... it is possible... it is yours."

—AYN RAND, *ATLAS SHRUGGED*

Contents

PART THREE—CARPE VITAM (SEIZE LIFE)

Forewarned is Forearmed

WILLIAM KEIPER'S BOOKS are wake-up calls. They all shine the light of reality onto the challenges of our society and offer solutions we can implement right away. His books are gifts to those who have the wisdom to find and read them.

When he asked me to read this manuscript as he was working on it, I was honored and excited because of how much I'd enjoyed his previous books. Until now, my favorites have been *Life Expectancy* and *The Power of Urgency.*

When I read *Untethered Aging*, it called up for me the wisdom of Miguel de Cervantes, "Forewarned; forearmed: to be prepared is half the victory." This book is a clearly stated forewarning for all seniors about the myriad challenges of aging and how to deal with them.

This book brings the same sense of reality and urgency that his others do, but it feels more personal to me. Maybe it's because it is about aging, and I'm in my own senior years. Or maybe it's because what it reveals shocked me out of my own lazy avoidance of the reality of our world and its meaning for me personally.

Keiper built his career as a business leader and later a business consultant by exercising his remarkable gift for critical analysis. He had the fearlessness to introduce his colleagues and clients to realities they either couldn't or wouldn't see for themselves. Along with often eye-opening revelations delivered with absolute candor, he consistently offered creative and highly actionable solutions.

He has successfully transferred these gifts in the real world of operating businesses to his work as an author. He has never done it as brilliantly as he has in this timely book.

Untethered Aging showed me the forest I couldn't see for the trees in terms of aging and its challenges and potential. More importantly, it gave me an innovative field manual for clearing my way to freedom in my senior years of living.

This meticulously researched book makes it dramatically clear how and why seniors are facing significant challenges. The rate of change in our lives has resulted in a world turned upside down by predatory technology, political divisiveness, worldwide viral diseases, and governmental incompetence. Our self-inflicted wounds have complicated it: living beyond our means and failing to save for our now-longer life expectancies.

Understanding these challenges has become an *urgent* necessity. For most people, the concept of urgency is rarely associated with creative power. It's most often aligned with fear, denial, and perhaps even a withdrawal from the field of play. But those who remain willingly ignorant will not find their senior years to be anywhere close to what used to be called the *golden years*.

This book offers a shockingly clear look at the realities of the world we now live in and a compelling action plan for seniors who cannot only "survive" the challenges but can wake up and thrive in ways they may never have been able to do in their earlier years.

He has made clear the 'why' and the 'how' for undertaking the enormous adaptation that seniors must make to survive and thrive throughout the remainder of their life expectancies.

The clear and inspiring choice on offer in these pages is the choice between aging with a renewed sense and spirit of freedom and creativity or aging in a powerless, frightening way, devoid of dignity and self-esteem.

The seniors suffering most will be those who are, as Keiper says, "tethered" to outdated and misguided beliefs that no longer serve them. They may continue to blindly trust that somehow or another, they will be taken care of in their later years. Keiper makes the irrefutable case that this is a false and dangerous assumption.

My dictionary's first definition of the word tether is a "...rope, strap, cord or chain for keeping an animal at a certain distance." The second definition is about us humans. A tether is "the extent or limit of our resources, abilities or endurance."

In my decades of work as a life coach and corporate trainer, it became clear that the limits we place on our "resources, abilities, and endurance" are more a function of our internal thoughts and beliefs than they are of external circumstances or past personal history. It's an inside job that we do to ourselves.

And as recent discoveries in neuroscience and positive psychology confirm, we are not hardwired to any kind of permanent personality traits and habits, no matter how much it looks and feels that way. We can develop new habits and personality pathways to alter what we are doing and change and upgrade *who we are being*.

I can "be" old, passive, mentally checked-out, and at the mercy of whichever government program or family members have the capacity and desire to take care of me. Or I can rise up, take on the challenges and thrive, making my last years the best years of my life. This book is the answer for the second option. The one that has me rising up!

On a personal note, as I write this, I am in my mid-seventies and still working full time. I have been experiencing vague anxieties and uncertainty about what my own final years will be like. What I hadn't expected was what an impact this book would have on me personally and how many positive changes and action plans it would inspire me to begin creating for my own "golden years." I'm so grateful for what *Untethered Aging* has shown me.

I'm glad you have the book now, whatever your age may be. My prediction is that you will like it as much as I do, and, like me, you'll want to share it with everyone you care about who is in... or entering... this surprisingly high-potential age group previously known as the elderly—people who were thought to be finished with life and just waiting passively through their senior years.

You can use this book—not as a way to finish—but to *begin* something new and fulfilling. If you take it in deeply (and accept my recommendation to read it more than once), you'll have a way to live the rest of your life untethered to any old beliefs about who you were and what you could do.

This invitation to *create* the rest of your life is the real gift of Keiper's work in *Untethered Aging*.

S T E V E C H A N D L E R
B I R M I N G H A M , M I C H I G A N
M A R C H 2021

A Twenty-Year Blur

THE FIRST TWO decades of the 21st century brought more change than any other period in history. The rise of digital technology dominated this transformation. The Tech Giants created compelling and seductive new social environments in the form of online communities. Adding to the disorder was the unexpected mayhem of the Covid-19 pandemic, the Great Recession, the 9/11 attacks, and many natural disasters.

Almost without our knowing, twenty years flew past. We were committed to the daily grind while attempting to drink from the firehose of change. Over 95 million U.S. adults ages 55 and older are confronting another significant challenge: aging through the once romanticized "Golden Years."

The pace of change, already incredible, will accelerate over the next twenty years. The things that once grounded us have given way, replaced not by better footing but by more uncertainty. No part of the population can ignore it. It will require adaptability from all, especially seniors for whom flexing with the times becomes more challenging.

Retirement used to mean a more relaxed life. In many cases, it also meant a time when retirement resources *exceeded* the needs for remaining then-shorter life expectancies. This surplus forestalled a sense of anxiety due to financial insufficiency. But the Boomer-led population explosion, coupled with significantly extended lifespans, has put pressure on all aspects of American senior living. For many, outliving financial resources is a concern greater than dying.

When your lifespan clock turns fifty-five, sixty, sixty-five, or even eighty-five, you may be at your best in many ways. This time is about freeing yourself from the social and psychological constraints that may have held you down. The stuff you may be dragging behind you is like memorabilia: the boxes are heavy, they take up a lot of room, and ultimately most of it will go in a dumpster.

Untethered aging is rediscovering self-reliance. It is choosing to deal rationally with that holding you back from achieving psychological freedom.

In Part One, *A New Normal*, we will explore the facts, meaning, and consequences of some of the significant macro-environmental factors. This exploration is an invitation to expand your worldview. Technological innovation, rate-of-change, and the Tech Giants' cultural dominance and power are among these elements.

In Part Two, *Your Money and Your Life*, we will address income sufficiency and the rising challenge of the affordability of necessities. You will learn about the pervasiveness of these factors across the entire American populace.

We will focus on the challenges for older Americans. Many on fixed incomes now feel uncertain about the reliability of institutions once viewed as trustworthy. I offer a highly actionable prescription for answering the question, "How will I live within my means for the rest of my life?" I will make the case that if you choose avoidance over action because you desire safety and security, your trust is misplaced

Part Three, *Carpe Vitam (Seize Life)*, is a pragmatic view of aging well while exploring individual significance. It is also a vehicle for discovering individual and collective purpose and meaning. We will explore the big existential questions, including "Who am I? and "Did I matter?" and ways to manage end-of-life concerns.

We must no longer accept the lie that declining relevance due to aging is inevitable. *Untethered Aging* explores how seniors can find value in longer lives, lived better, and how to effectively deal with the perpetual challenges of financial sufficiency and physical well-being. It provides a roadmap for reaching psychological freedom through *creating* the rest of your life.

PART ONE

A New Normal

Chapter 1

The Bigger Picture

SEEING THE WORLD around us for what it is can be depressing. It requires a little faith. Alan Watts said an attitude of faith is to let go and become open to truth, whatever it might turn out to be. We will first explore some of the influential forces in the world around us. This reality check is necessary to discover the freedom and fulfillment that is the essence of untethered aging.

Our world's primary macro factors and forces include the physical and ecological, demographic, technological, economic, political, legal, and social. From time-to-time, I will collectively refer to these as the *Bigger Picture* factors. They are of such enormity and complexity that bending them to favor one person, or even a determined group, is mostly futile.

Most of these influences today are unique in their speed, complexity, and degree of impact. They have become sources of widespread stress, anxiety, and uncertainty. Most have been made more severe due to individual actions taken against our collective best interests. One example of our anti-humanity behaviors is the widespread degradation of environmental biodiversity.

We not only inhabit our minds and bodies but the world outside of us. The sobering truth about our external environment will provide a foundation for making better decisions in our habitats closer to home.

"When the bad news starts pouring in—whether reporting crimes in a city, medical errors in a hospital, or new patient cases in a pandemic—this actually means you've jumped over your first hurdle to success. With accurate information, people can turn their attention and skills to the challenges of developing novel solutions to the newly visible problems... [rather] than living with false confidence that all is well..."[1]

Be curious about what is going on in the world-at-large, and you will see your environment differently. You will envision options and opportunities that you would swear were not there before.

Put into the context of Reinhold Niebuhr's *Serenity Prayer*, these Bigger Picture factors are things that wisdom will guide us to conclude we cannot change.[2] We should reserve our courage and energy for changing the things we can with as much force as we can muster.

Every person should be familiar with the significant drivers of the world in which we live and use that knowledge to navigate its complexity and challenges better. We must arm ourselves with more knowledge than ever to adapt our living to the speed of change and its continuous acceleration.

---

1. Source: https://hbr.org/2020/03/dont-hide-bad-news-in-times-of-crisis
2. Source: https://en.wikipedia.org/wiki/Serenity_Prayer

Chapter 2

The Obvious Truth

I SERVED AS CEO, President, and board member for companies listed on the NYSE and NASDAQ exchanges and smaller private businesses for most of my career. Most of them were part of the digital technology business sector. Strategy, urgent change, and complex problem solving were at the center of my working life.

My friend and mentor, Steve Chandler, wrote this about me in the foreword to my book, *The Power of Urgency: Playing to Win with Proactive Urgency,*

> When I first met Will Keiper, I thought he had a bit of a problem. He wasn't a very good compromiser. His preference was to challenge go-along-to-get-along company cultures and people. He was a man on the move, and he sometimes came off as impatient. Some called him 'brutally honest,' with the emphasis on the 'brutal' part. He would call it, getting to the *'obvious truth.'* I later learned that what he had wasn't a problem at all. He had a special kind of objectivity and sense of urgency that was his alone. It was how he knew to be most effective. He preferred results—and rapidly.

I believe that people can do things differently when they can see them differently. Urgent change is possible once 'what we know' is challenged.

Your unique creativity can be engaged and deliver you from the status quo.

As an executive, business consultant, and author, my professional career success has been based upon my ability to shift perspectives. I vigorously challenge history and assumptions that are no longer valid. This process includes identifying the 'what and why' of people being unwilling or unable to look hard at what is no longer working. The discovery and examination of the 'obvious truth' is a required step in breaking down the door to reinvention.

Distinguishing today's perceptions and thoughts from the feelings we attach to them can become more challenging as we age. As seniors observing a new event or condition, we may say to ourselves, "I know what this is, I've seen it before, and I don't like it." This reaction can come up even before we have assessed all the facts. But characterizing attributes as "good" or "bad" typically is of little value in problem-solving. This emotional response becomes an immediate hurdle to the discovery of potential creative solutions.

Rational thinking is based upon the discovery of objective reality as best it can be determined. It is acting in a manner that is life-preserving and goal-achieving. You cannot eliminate emotion, but rational observations and reactions serve us better in most cases. This foundation is even more valuable for dealing with the blur of external change referenced in the Introduction.

Unsurprisingly, my methods cause some pain. I insist on confronting questions that might make for some temporary discomfort. Some unease in discovering the answers to be different than you thought is part of it. I call it the *good pain* necessary for any breakthrough.

You know about good pain. It is a part of the process of improving your physical fitness level, restructuring your lifestyle to save money, or transforming a business. There is always a level of anxiety felt when moving from the safe harbor of the status quo into the less-forgiving ocean just outside it.

Hearing about the nature of my skills and experience, you might think that I would know how to avoid staying stuck. The sense of fragility, disillusionment, fear, and uncertainty you will read about in *Untethered Aging* is a mirror of my feelings. My story of the past decade or so includes one major life challenge following another.

I gave up the most personally and financially rewarding position of my career because I did not recognize a change in attitude and circumstances against my best interest. Shortly after that, eighty percent of my net worth disappeared in the unforgiving aftermath of the Great Recession. During this period, I went through a costly divorce followed by a too-fast entry into another unsuccessful and emotionally painful marriage.

In the aftermath of the breakage, I moved across the country for a consulting engagement. I spent two years in an organization led by a man whose philosophy of leadership was reminiscent of the great quote from Jim Rohn, "There are two ways to have the tallest building in town. One is to tear everyone else's building down, and the other is to build yours taller." This man could only see one option, and it was the first. I found myself in a perpetually stressful environment.

Add to those events the pain of losing treasured animal companions. I had to say goodbye to Ozzie, a 17-year-old white toy poodle, and Lou, a 14-year-old, long-haired gray Nebelung cat. With all due respect for human relationships, I have always appreciated the four-legged companions in my life.[3] Since the stilling of theirs, my heartbeat seems louder—a metronome reminding me of the beat-by-beat passage of my life.

---

3. Sidonie-Gabrielle Colette, a French author, wrote, "Our perfect companions never have fewer than four feet."

Chapter 3

Life Expectancy

MY FIRST BOOK was titled *Life Expectancy: It's Never Too Late to Change Your Game.* The outer boundary of my life came into my awareness as I researched and wrote it. I started asking questions such as, "How much time do I have?" "What should I do with it?" and "How will I feel about how and with whom I spend my time now when there is less of it later?"

We cannot comprehend the concepts of time, aging, and lifetime on the day of our births. We cannot convert our probable life expectancy of about 75 to 80 years into the number of days (about 29,200).[4] If we could have formed such thoughts, we probably would have viewed that time as virtually unlimited.

As we come to understand time in hours, days, months, and years, we give little notice to the lengthening runway behind us. We likely give even less thought to the outer limit of our time on Earth, the runway ahead.

We live through periods of growing up, being educated, taking first steps into the workplace, relationships, perhaps marriage and children, and a career. We prioritize making a living, raising kids, managing

---

4. Life expectancies at birth calculate the average lifespan for everybody who was born in the same year.

work and home relationships, and tending to our social media and other connections. Almost everything outside of those insistent and incessant requirements gets kicked down the road when "we'll have more time."

I gave the commencement address on the fortieth anniversary of my graduation from Eastern Illinois University. I decided to highlight the limited allotment of days of life in urging the graduates to reflect on their life passages periodically.

As I looked out over the audience, I said, "When I was your age and sitting where you are, it was forty years ago today. Just like you, I had used a quarter of my life (about 7,300 days) getting here."

I continued, "As of now, I have spent 21,900 of my life-days, about 75 percent of them. The good news is you have about three-quarters of your full life expectancy remaining. You can choose to spend it more consciously, starting now." The rest of the speech was about how quickly those years would pass.

What I did not say on that happy night was that all things being equal, between 10 and 15 percent of them will die by the age of 65.[5]

Uttering those words about my diminishing lifespan rang in my ears. I did not *feel* far removed from wearing the cap and gown. However, my allotment of living days at the time of the graduation ceremony had declined to 8,760. Now, in my 70th year, my remaining days have been reduced to about 3,650.[6]

---

5. Source: https://data.worldbank.org/indicator/SP.DYN.TO65.MA.ZS?locations =US
6. As we live longer, our life expiration dates are extended. A man surviving to age 70, as have I, can expect to live another 14.39 years, or 5,252 days, all things being equal. Source: https://www.ssa.gov/oact/STATS/table4c6.html

You probably do not periodically calculate the likely number of days remaining to you. If you did, would you approach your time, commitments, activities, and even thoughts differently? Internalizing it might represent motivation for how you choose to create the rest of your life and with what degree of urgency.

In the balance of *Untethered Aging*, I offer my assessment of our living context today and a practical vision for the successful creation of a richer rest-of-your-life. It represents a how-to approach for freeing yourself from preconceived notions about aging and expanding your thinking about what is possible.

Chapter 4

Alone in a Sea of Humanity

EARTH'S HUMAN POPULATION is approaching eight billion. It was about 2.5 billion in the middle of last century's Baby Boom. The U.S. population has more than doubled since then, to about 331 million. There are now over 95 million U.S. adults ages 55 and older. This cohort represents about 28 percent of the total U.S. population. Those of us now part of the global senior community make up a significant number of the billions of the microdots creating the extraordinary spike in the population growth curve.[7]

The world population increases annually by about 82 million (roughly equivalent to the people of Germany). But the number of the Earth's human inhabitants will not double, let alone quadruple, this century.[8] Today's annual birth rate is less than 50 percent of what it was in 1968 (the peak of the Baby Boom) and will continue to fall through the year 2100.

---

7. Source: Public Domain https://commons.wikimedia.org/w/index.php?curid=1355720 Author note: From time-to-time, I use charts and other graphical depictions to reinforce the points I am making my best effort to describe for you in words. For me, written information presented with visual support has more impact than just reading or seeing. All datasets were independently sourced and attributed to the providers. They were not verified independently by me, though I have made my best effort to crosscheck other sources to confirm their general reliability. The charts and graphs are offered as guides though, not gospel.
8. Source: http://www.transgenerational.org/aging/demographics.htm#ixzz1Qh M6YOFy

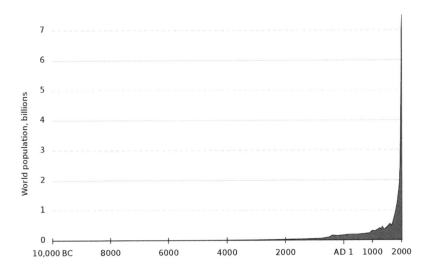

We live much longer than was projected when we were born. The average life expectancy for an American born in 1950 was 65.6 years, and in 2020, over 79. A person now reaching 65 can expect to live to about 84, all things being equal.[9] (Anecdotally, the life expectancy for U.S. men and women in 1900 was 46.8 and 48.8 years, respectively.)

This life extension was an unexpected gift, rising extraordinarily over a single generation. Many complications have resulted, including significant affordability challenges, rising healthcare costs, and uneven social well-being. We were not ready to live into our 80s on average, had not saved for it, and haven't yet figured out how to cope with it at scale. Two of its consequences are financial fragility and more significant stress during the now extended twilight years.

We also have witnessed a greater degree of individual isolation. In part, this separation is a consequence of the attention demanded by smartphones, apps, and the always-on world of the internet.

---

9. Source: https://www.prb.org/aging-unitedstates-fact-sheet

Online social platforms such as Facebook, Twitter, and Instagram, once heralded as new communities bringing people together have done the opposite. The 'connections' are touches on a screen or keypad (or a voice) to issue communications or commands through the device. Where's the community? But we persistently engage as though we are part of one, taking time and attention away from almost everything else.

Social communities also have become significant sources of misinformation and disinformation. They have enabled the widespread and largely unregulated distribution of divisive content, adding to our sense of distance from others. Users intent on this kind of disruption have had a significant impact on individual mental and physical health, creating even more isolation.[10]

Social Media = Positive & Negative

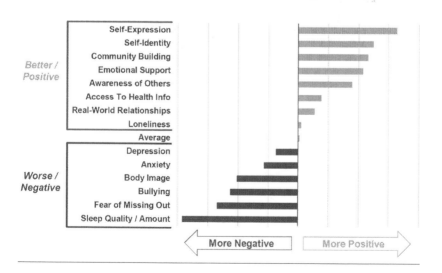

Do Social Media Platforms You Use Make These Health-Related Factors Better or Worse?

---

10. Source: Royal Society for Public Health survey of 1,479 British teens

A 2020 report from the National Academies of Sciences, Engineering, and Medicine (NASEM) concluded that more than one-third of adults aged 45 and older feel lonely.[11] One-fourth of adults 65 and older are socially isolated. I believe these numbers are significantly understated and will get progressively worse. In a world filled with more people than ever before, is an epidemic of isolation.

Older adults are at increased risk for loneliness because they are more likely to live alone, have lost family and friends through death or estrangement, have developed chronic illnesses, and suffer hearing loss due to aging.[12] The NASEM report offers strong evidence that many adults ages 50 and older are socially isolated or lonely in ways that put their health at risk.

Recent studies found that:

- Social isolation significantly increases a person's risk of premature death from all causes, rivaling smoking, obesity, and physical inactivity.
- It was associated with about a 50 percent increase in the risk of dementia.
- Poor social relationships (from social isolation or loneliness) were associated with a 29 percent increased risk of heart disease and a 32 percent higher stroke risk.
- Loneliness was also associated with higher rates of depression, anxiety, and suicide.
- Studies found a nearly four times higher risk of death and a 68 percent greater risk of hospitalization attributable to isolation. Among heart failure patients, these conditions drove a 57 percent higher risk of emergency room visits.

---

11. Source: https://www.pewresearch.org/fact-tank/2019/07/03/on-average-older-adults-spend-over-half-their-waking-hours-alone/
12. Source: https://www.cdc.gov/aging/publications/features/lonely-older-adults.html

A meta-analysis from Brigham Young University followed 3.4 million people over an average of seven years. This study found the likelihood of dying increased by 26 percent for people who reported feeling lonely, 29 percent for socially isolated participants, and 32 percent for those who lived alone.

The Covid-19 pandemic has significantly increased individual, family, and community isolation and has spared no generations.

Relatedness becomes more critical as we age.[13] In addition to the physical effects, the absence of person-to-person connections can bring up feelings of irrelevance and insignificance. The potential for depression is associated with such losses of self-esteem.

In Chapter 28, "Social Self-Reliance—Trusting in Others," and in Chapter 29, "The Wellness Forum," we will address ways to reach out to others to support your physical, psychological, and relatedness needs.

---

13. Source: "Correlates and Predictors of Loneliness in Older Adults: A Review of Quantitative Results Informed by Qualitative Insights," *International Psychogeriatric Journal*, 2016 Apr 28 (4) 557-76

Chapter 5

Change at the Speed of Light

COMPUTERS HAVE DOUBLED their capabilities every twelve to eighteen months for decades. This progress has powered an unrelenting stream of innovations that rely upon them. Over just the past twenty years, the technology and devices designed and developed to serve humans have expanded at a rate almost beyond comprehension.

The creation of the Internet (the "internet") was a landmark breakthrough in digital technology history. Its architectural system, the World Wide Web (the "web"), was made available to the public on August 6, 1991. On that date, Tim Berners-Lee, credited as the driving force of the internet's development, posted a summary of the project for all the world to see.[14] Since then, this technology platform has been chief among the enablers of global knowledge expansion.

Google made the internet universally accessible. Its introduction of an organizational and search scheme for website locations and their content made it possible for anyone to navigate the online universe. Through merely asking a question, you will instantly be delivered answers. In most cases, lots of them. For example, "Okay, Google, what is biodiversity?" If you make this inquiry, you will receive about 80,000,000 reference points in half a second.

---

14. Source: https://thenextweb.com/insider/2011/08/06/20-years-ago-today-the-world-wide-web-opened-to-the-public/

There are over 4.8 billion users of the web today, accessing over 1.8 billion websites.[15] Both measures rise every second of every day. Google now receives over seven billion search requests each day.

The companies described below introduced products that changed the world in just the *first ten years* of the 21st century. Their brand names are internationally renowned, and their products and technologies integrated into our daily lives: iPod (2001), Wikipedia (2001), Skype (2003), Facebook (2004), YouTube (2005), Twitter (2006), Nintendo Wii (2006), the first iPhone (2007), Amazon Kindle (2007), and the iPad (2010). We have also seen the introduction and refinement of Bluetooth, GPS, the cloud, file sharing, hybrid cars, human genome sequencing, online streaming, the birth control patch, 3D printing, multi-use rockets, self-driving cars, the robotic heart, and many, many more.[16]

The chart below estimates the improvement level that our technology will have during the next five years. It *almost* seems manageable at a multiplier of 32 times, considering our adaptation over the past 20 years.[17]

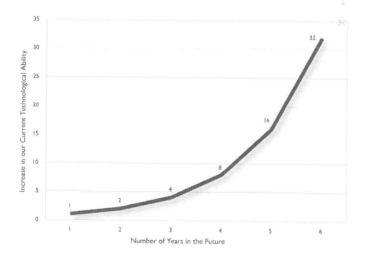

15. Source: https://www.websitehostingrating.com/internet-statistics-facts/
16. Source: https://www.usatoday.com/story/money/2020/01/09/21-most-important-inventions-of-the-21st-century/40934825/
17. Source: http://www.theemergingfuture.com/speed-technological-advancement .htm

It isn't nearly as easy to fathom what will be required to cope with an expected million times greater technology advancement over the next twenty years.[18]

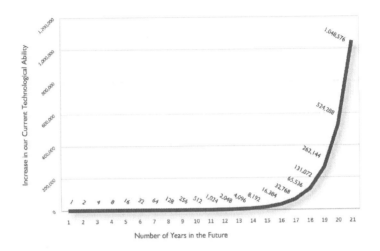

Most charts representing the rate of technological change in our lifetimes have shapes like the ones just above. Humans are always found somewhere in the vapor trails of the rockets transporting us to the future.[19] However, ultimately, we do adapt. Humans invented, advanced, and now manage and direct these digital technologies and many others.[20]

It is not beyond any of us to remain connected and active in the digital world. Despite the points made earlier about isolation, digital connections also represent bridges. We will have access to incredible and diverse resources to help us navigate the years ahead, even if seniors trail others' adaptation rate.

---

18. Source: http://www.theemergingfuture.com/speed-technological-advancement-twenty-years.htm
19. Source: https://miro.medium.com/max/4094/1*At2fvrfdtXOOw7a8Gy4VMg.png
20. Source: https://blogs.sap.com/2017/07/27/machine-learning-thursdays-evolution-in-the-age-of-acceleration/

Our brains still have more raw computing power than the world's fastest supercomputers (for the moment).[21] Computers with a million processors can only approach a small percentage of the human brain's processing capability. And that requires a lot of simplifying assumptions. A few hundred neuron transmissions occurring in our brains can accomplish the same calculations that might take a computer a few million steps.

The amount of energy required to drive computations by the world's fastest supercomputer is enough to power a building. The human brain achieves the same processing speeds from the electricity needed for light bulb illumination.[22] If we need something to help us adapt to the pace of change, we will use our intelligence to invent and learn how to use it.

Danah Boyd, a Senior Researcher at Microsoft Research, said, "Technology forces disruption, and not all of the change will be good. Optimists look to all the excitement. Pessimists look to all that gets lost. They're both right. How you react depends on what you have to gain versus what you have to lose."[23] The lives of seniors will be vastly richer by embracing new devices and apps with curiosity and positive expectations. There is much to gain.

Another reason to be an optimist regarding technology is that we have proven for billions of years our capacity for dealing with any change. Each of us now walking the Earth has this built-in capability.

Human brains also have the advantage and flexibility of adapting their structures. When the brain identifies a more efficient or effective way

---

21. Source: https://www.scientificamerican.com/article/a-new-supercomputer-is-the-worlds-fastest-brain-mimicking-machine/
22. Source: https://www.scienceabc.com/humans/the-human-brain-vs-super com puters-which-one-wins.html
23. Source: https://www.fastcompany.com/1802732/generation-flux-meet-pioneers-new-and-chaotic-frontier-business

to compute and function, it can morph and alter its physical and neu-
ronal structure. This capacity is called neuroplasticity and is uniquely
human.[24]

Neuroscientists once thought that neuroplasticity manifested only during
childhood. Scientists have now concluded that some brain processes
can adapt throughout adulthood. You were born with this ability and
can engage it without an operating manual.

As aging Americans, we have access to a universe of digital, medical,
biological, genetic, and many other technology-based solutions. Our
future will never be about staying the same. It can't and won't and is a
blessing. We can explore the world from wherever we are and never
worry about boredom.

------

24. Source: https://en.wikipedia.org/wiki/Neuroplasticity

Chapter 6

The Tech Giants

THE TECH GIANTS responsible for the innovations referenced in Chapter 5 have exploded in visibility and value.[25] These social, cultural, and economic titans have shown that it is possible to thrive in environments where the only constant is change. As a reward, they have become the most valuable businesses in the world.[26]

Over the past fifteen years, the Tech Giants have displaced all but one on a list of the world's eight most valuable businesses. Apple was not on this roster in 2005 but now is at the top, followed by Amazon, Microsoft, Alphabet (Google), and Facebook. Together, these five companies represent almost one-fifth of the value of all the others in the S&P 500 index. They have become indispensable for our adaptation to a head-spinning rate of change in nearly all living aspects.

These companies have this in common: Embracing rapid transformation as a way of doing business is not something to resist. They are fierce about being *their* agents of change. They accomplish *creative destruction* before others force it.[27]

---

25. Source: https://www.statista.com/chart/22677/the-age-of-the-tech-giants/
26. Source: https://www.statista.com/chart/17545/worlds-most-profitable-companies/
27. Joseph Schumpeter, an American economist and sociologist known for his theories of capitalist development and business cycles, called creative destruction a desirable culling of businesses that cannot keep pace.

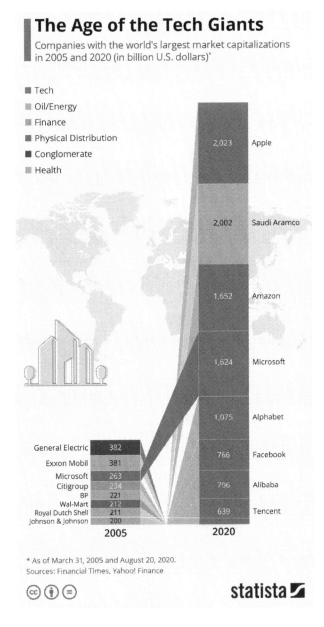

The Age of the Tech Giants

Companies with the world's largest market capitalizations
in 2005 and 2020 (in billion U.S. dollars)*

- Tech
- Oil/Energy
- Finance
- Physical Distribution
- Conglomerate
- Health

2020

2,023	Apple
2,002	Saudi Aramco
1,652	Amazon
1,624	Microsoft
1,075	Alphabet
766	Facebook
706	Alibaba
639	Tencent

2005

Company	Value
General Electric	382
Exxon Mobil	381
Microsoft	263
Citigroup	234
BP	221
Wal-Mart	212
Royal Dutch Shell	211
Johnson & Johnson	200

* As of March 31, 2005 and August 20, 2020.
Sources: Financial Times, Yahoo! Finance

statista

These Tech Giants have become so dominant and powerful that the U.S. and other governments are concerned. The economic, market, social, and cultural power of these companies has brought antitrust charges and the potential for greater regulation. The companies have significantly raised their voices in the corridors of Washington, D.C., and elsewhere to slow it down.

The Tech Giants' products and platforms are essential to human connection, social expression, business, government, communication, and influence worldwide. Although the human pace of adaptation will always trail technical innovations, we have proven our ability over time to use them in practical ways.

All generations, including many senior Americans, now use systems and products that once seemed beyond their grasp. We have embraced smartphones and other computing devices, social networks, apps, gaming, online shopping and banking, video streaming, and conferencing. We are using many other things that we could not have foreseen when growing up with landline phones, pencils, and record players.

The Tech Giants have driven enormous value by creating and distributing digital technology and products. Technology represents a set of tools for living in and mastering the sped-up world that challenges all of us. Transformation against the odds is in your DNA with an assist from neuroplasticity. Whether you realized it or not, you have been rapidly and successfully mastering an unprecedentedly dynamic environment.

We do not have access to the same management skills, people, or resources, as the Tech Giants. However, we can move with greater urgency in both decision-making and action. Our knowledge of the Bigger Picture factors and a sense of urgency focused on adaptation can help us deal with an unrelenting stream of change.

No matter your life stage, the ability to see things differently and embrace change requires a new kind of psychological resilience. If you spend time justifying why you are not up to shifting some of your thoughts and actions, you may find yourself further behind than you were a moment ago. This proactivity is self-reliance, a set of values we will explore in-depth.

Chapter 7

Online Anonymity and Trust

THE DIGITAL WEB and its social networks and communities have overtaken our earthly lives. When online, humans are hidden behind screens and lost in layers and layers of digital infrastructure. Although access and knowledge are precious commodities, device-to-device connections have reduced face-to-face communication and relatedness. Social networks have displaced a large percentage of our real-life family time and community involvement.

The question for many is, "Where does my real-life end and my online persona begin?" They are inextricably intertwined. Who would have expected we could enter and extend our life experience into an entire alternate reality. With a single click, our universe now includes unlimited online social connections.

Without knowing the difference, you could be engaging with a legitimate new 'friend,' business connection, or potential romantic interest. However, it is just as likely to be a cybercriminal, scammer, or one of an army of non-human digital imposters. It is almost impossible to know. Made-up names and profiles, fake accounts, false histories, and gender impersonation are part of the counterfeit digital landscape.

In an alternate social world where anonymity virtually eliminates personal accountability and consequences, why not try your hand at acting? Behind your digital mask, you can choose to be real, fictitious, or anonymous. You can reveal nothing or everything. You can post personal photos or those of someone whose likeness you select to portray as yours. You can choose to disclose the best of your humanity or hide every shred of it. You can be whoever you want to be now and another digital incarnation later, or even simultaneously. Many multiple personalities can exist in the digital cosmos.

The limited trust factor that we often freely offer in initial real-life connections is inappropriate online. Yet many of us continue taking what we know about real-world humanity, the paradigms of authentication, trust, confidence, kindness, and empathy, and apply them to the virtual world. They do not translate. Ironically, the more time and attention we spend in online communities, the more we distance ourselves from our humanness. We may even adopt behaviors in real life that are acceptable online when anonymous but antisocial (or worse) when seen in natural light.

The demand for attention from our mobile devices has dramatically cut into the time we could be interacting with others, even those in the same room. If you are thinking, "This only relates to younger people," you are wrong. Even those 60 and older are giving more-and-more time to their collection of screens.[28] The average American adult commits over 35 percent of their attention during waking hours to online activities. This time commitment is more than we spend watching television, listening to music, and gaming, combined. We are isolating ourselves in place by choice. If there is anybody around us, they are likely doing the same thing.

---

28. Source: https://www.pewresearch.org/fact-tank/2019/06/18/americans-60-and-older-are-spending-more-time-in-front-of-their-screens-than-a-decade-ago/

The ultimate objective of the social platform Tech Giants is a monopoly.[29] A monopoly of your attention for 100 percent of your waking hours, or about two-thirds of your life. There are probably plans, if not existing solutions, for owning your attention during your sleeping hours as well. More than two-thirds of the adult population already have their smartphones within arm's reach while sleeping. We are assisting the Tech Giants in conquering the final attention frontier—our sleeping hours.

We have unlimited access to our online world wherever we are: at home, work, studying, dining with friends, at family gatherings, and traveling. A step in the right direction is setting boundaries for online activities. Many parents limit their children's online time, viewable sites, and types of communication. As adults, we could learn from this kind of parental management and impose some limitations on ourselves.

The number of worldwide smartphone users now surpasses three billion. It is forecasted to grow by several hundred million more in the next few years. China, India, and the United States are the countries with the highest number of smartphone users.[30] Worldwide, more people now own a cell phone than a toothbrush.[31]

Seniors are increasingly adopting smartphones as their devices of choice, too. A 2019 Pew Research study found that 68 percent of Baby Boomers own smartphones, and 52 percent own tablets. It undoubtedly is rising each year.

29. Source: https://www.nytimes.com/interactive/2020/10/06/technology/house-antitrust-report-big-tech.html?action=click&module=RelatedLinks&pgtype=Article and https://www.nytimes.com/2020/10/06/technology/congress-big-tech-monopoly-power.html?campaign_id=60&emc=edit_na_20201006&instance_id=0&nl=breaking-news&ref=cta&regi_id=71137299&segment_id=40001&user_id=35b257850e9ca3ae364e7d273f248909
30. Source: https://www.statista.com/statistics/330695/number-of-smartphone-users-worldwide/
31. Source: https://review42.com/smartphone-statistics/

While in the alternate reality of our online adventures, we cannot give full attention to those who might deserve it or even pay for it. Two examples of those short-changed include employers and family members. Many prefer to surrender other people and activities in their lives than be without their smartphones. For confirmation of this, observe any family of four while dining in a restaurant. It is a rarity not to see some or all the group actively or passively engaged with their smartphones, leaving the others attention-starved around the dinner table.

Chapter 8

When Addiction is Normal

THE SMARTPHONE IS a very demanding attention sucker. An average user touches it 2,617 times every day. The extreme users—the top ten percent—touch them over 5,400 times daily.[32] Could the smartphone as a versatile utility device be at the core of a culturally accepted personal addiction?

Let's take a look at casino gaming for some clues.[33] Eighty percent of Las Vegas revenues come from one-on-one encounters with machines, not social play around a table. The ability to engage with slot machines uninterrupted is one of the underlying reasons. Natasha Dow Schull, the author of *Addiction by Design: Machine Gambling in Las Vegas*, said, "Playing on slot machines is solitary, rapid and continuous. You don't have interruptions like you would in a live poker game, waiting for cards to be dealt or waiting for the other players. You can go directly from one hand to the next—there's no clear stopping point built into the game. You don't even have to stop to put bills in the machine; the machines take credit or barcoded tickets."

---

32. Sources: https://www.journals.uchicago.edu/doi/abs/10.1086/691462?journalCode=jacr and https://blog.dscout.com/mobile-touches

33. Source: https://newrepublic.com/article/115838/gambling-addiction-why-are-slot-machines-so-addictive

The similarities between using smartphones to access social media and the addictive elements of casino and internet gaming are unmistakable. It is a war to get and keep your attention on the screen and away from everything else. This objective is top-of-mind in building new phones, apps, and games.

Maya MacGuineas, president of the Committee for a Responsible Federal Budget, wrote in *The Atlantic,*

> A generation of Silicon Valley executives trained at the Stanford Behavior Design Lab in the Orwellian art of manipulating the masses. The lab's founder, the experimental psychologist B. J. Fogg, has isolated the elements necessary to keep users of an app, a game, or a social network coming back for more.

> The buzzes, badges, and streaks of social media; the personalized "deals" of commerce sites; the camaraderie and thrilling competition of gaming; the algorithmic precision of the recommendations on YouTube—all have been finely tuned to keep us coming back for more. And we are: The average person taps, types, swipes, and clicks on his smartphone 2,617 times a day. Ninety-three percent of people sleep with their devices within arm's reach. Seventy-five percent use them in the bathroom.

In *Hooked: How to Build Habit-Forming Products*, an influential manual for developers, Nir Eyal describes enticement benefits, including variable rewards.[34] Think of the rush of anticipation you experience as you wait for your Twitter feed to refresh, hoping to see new likes and replies. Introducing such rewards to an app or a game, Eyal says, "...suppresses the areas of the brain associated with judgment and reason while activating the parts associated with wanting and desire."

---

34. Source: https://www.amazon.com/Hooked-How-Build-Habit-Forming-Products/dp/1591847788

For example, the brief lag between refresh and reveal is not Twitter crunching data—it's an intentional delay written into the code, designed to elicit the responses Eyal describes.

Maya MacGuineas concluded, "American society has long treated habit-forming products differently from non-habit-forming ones… but Big Tech has largely been left alone to insinuate addictive, potentially harmful products into the daily lives of millions of Americans, including children, by giving them away for free and even posturing as if they are a social good."[35]

The chairman of the Diagnostic and Statistical Manual for Mental Disorders task force (DSM-IV), and a Professor Emeritus at Duke University, Allen Frances, wrote, "Most of us spend a good part of our days in front of a screen, both professionally and recreationally. For many, the first and last act of the day is on a screen, with multiple interactions through the day and in the middle of the night… Are we all addicted?… If taken beyond its narrowest usage, 'behavioral addiction' would expand the definition of mental disorder to its breaking point and *would threaten to erase the concept of normality.*"[36]

The Tech Giants' goal was to keep our attention glued to the devices we use to access the web. They have achieved this objective other than for the remainder of our sleeping hours. Could all this effort be an end in itself? There is more to the story, and it begins with, "Follow the money…"

---

35. Source: https://www.theatlantic.com/magazine/archive/2020/04/capitalisms-addiction-problem/606769/

36. Source: https://www.rehabs.com/pro-talk/behavioral-addictions-a-dangerous-slippery-slope/

Chapter 9

Your Online Dossier:
A Penny for Your Behavioral Profile

ADDICTION TO THE device and the apps was only the first step for the Tech Giants. The second and much more richly rewarding one has been monetization. The source of their enormous cash flow and value is knowing where, when, and how users will spend their attention and money.

The terms and conditions that we mindlessly approve permit the social platform companies to follow our digital tracks. They operate online vacuum cleaners that suck up the details of where you have been, everything you have done, not done that you usually do, and for how long. It is like having someone following you around, capturing the DNA you leave in your physical wake.

Your digital details are consolidated, compiled, and curated as a digital life dossier with your name on it. The description of this activity by the platform companies is not as straightforward as this. Some social platform companies say with unmistakable irony,

> *...to better serve you,* we employ "... cognitive technologies, such as machine learning, neural networks, robotic process automation, bots, natural language processing, neural nets, and the broader domain of AI [artificial intelligence] ... These technologies personalize and contextualize the human-technology

interaction, allowing businesses to provide tailored language and image-based information and services, with minimal or no human involvement."[37] [Emphasis added.]

This disclosure is both numbing and poetic in the use of information technology terms we may have heard, but they know we do not understand.

The social media companies continuously track, compile, match, predict, construct, and deconstruct the 'you' that you do not know as well as they do.[38] The digital you—the one built-up from your online decisions and actions, millisecond-by-millisecond, click-by-click. Accepting a friend request or not, how long you looked at a specific photo or an ad before moving on, and your next online landing spot. The result of this process is their version of your behavioral profile.

Using it, a custom collection of the products, services, ideas, candidates, causes, and anything else the advertisers believe might grab your attention, will be displayed on your screen. They target you based upon insider-type insights about your well-being, stability, predispositions, vices, and the details of your spending (and most other) habits.

A case in point: I recently searched online for a slam ball to use for fitness training at home. It is a rubber-coated ball (typically weighted with sand) used in a range of physical conditioning exercises. After that, and no matter what website or page I went to, ads appeared for slam balls of all kinds. I had no idea there were so many colors, weights, sizes, and cover materials. These reminders were no accident.

---

37. Source: https://www2.deloitte.com/us/en/insights/focus/tech-trends/2020/macro-technology-trends.html#infographic

38. For highly interesting and understandable introductions to the science of this process, see the short documentaries, *The Creepy Line* www.thecreepyline.com and *The Social Dilemma* www.thesocialdilemma.com

Someone was paying for the privilege of knowing that I clicked some-where to learn about slam balls. Even if I only inadvertently found an article about them, I created a system input in a sea of billions or tril-lions of other bits of information, indicating that I might spend money on a slam ball. Ultimately, I bought one, perhaps because of the con-stant reminders I once thought it was a good idea. Judging from the amount of dust on it, I probably would have forgotten about 'needing it' and saved some money in the absence of the continuous prompts.

For your ad view, Facebook, Google, and other social platforms receive a few cents (or fractions thereof). You are a tiny but essential cog in a massive digital revenue and profit machine based upon the receipt of a few cents for a bit of your attention. With your permission, this is what they are selling to advertisers.

Multiply the mere pennies of revenue your views generate by billions (more likely, trillions). By any measure, it is real money. Most of these social media icons are public companies. You can check out their finan-cial results by searching online. Undoubtedly, they will add to your dossier the fact that you made that inquiry.

All your clicks, likes, links, and emojis reveal your state of well-being. You do not have to expressly indicate that there is something you want, as in the case of the slam ball. Your tracks may suggest that you might be stressed out. Soon, an ad for a Hawaiian holiday appears on your screen (that happens to be affordable based upon your previous spend-ing patterns). You say to yourself, "Wow, that is so weird. I've been feeling like I could use a vacation."

If you go, it may seem this was your idea and decision, but it probably was not. And it is not magic. It is information captured, sorted, and put together based upon where you place your attention, acted upon by an algorithm. It is leveraging your behaviors to pick your pocket with your consent. In this case, the result might have been that you went on a discretionary trip that reduced your bank account. The offers made based upon your behavioral profile may have nudged you into the decision.

When you consented to the terms and conditions, you gave up the right to keep private your most personal information: how you think, behave, and where you direct your attention. You give your digital world more and more and more of your time and attention because "...the new powers in the digital age have built their business models on strategies... [designed] to create a dependency on their products."[39]

Tristan Harris is the president and co-founder of the Center for Humane Technology.[40] He studied the ethics of human persuasion at Stanford and worked as a design ethicist at Google. He was interviewed in the docudrama *The Social Dilemma*. He said that the Tech Giants "... are not overwhelming our strengths, they are exploiting our weaknesses." Our behaviors are the tells revealed in our digital tracks, not our visible features nor what we say to others.

The social platforms compile your social and behavioral tracks. They push things to you based on what you will most likely act upon or buy. The companies' foremost objective is to keep you online for as long as possible. The middlemen are the companies paying for the ads. The ultimate beneficiaries are the company owners and shareholders. As in most mysteries, the game is fully revealed by following the money.

If this strategy and activity is not an existential threat to our culture and society, what is it? Even if these Tech Giants were willing to agree to some checks and balances, how could they be enforced? The ultimate black box is an artificial intelligence algorithm controlled by a few, or

---

39. Source: https://www.theatlantic.com/magazine/archive/2020/04/capitalisms-addiction-problem/606769/ https://www.scientificamerican.com/article/will-democracy-survive-big-data-and-artificial-intelligence/
40. Source: https://www.humanetech.com/

worse, another indecipherable algorithm. It is not tangible. It does not sit on a desk somewhere, and it is evolving by the second.

What if you were a government regulator or enforcer responsible for rebalancing power between social platform host and customer? The data bunkers of these companies are unfathomable rabbit holes. Imagine a black hole in space, a spacetime region where gravity is so strong that not even particles of light can escape it. If you enter, you may never make it out. Welcome to a Tech Giant computing center.

Our democratic society could begin to look more like China's totalitarian state, where a Citizen Score procedure is in process. "All [Chinese] citizens will be rated on a one-dimensional ranking scale. Everything they do gives plus or minus points... The score depends on an individual's clicks on the Internet and whether their conduct is politically correct or not. This determines their credit terms, their access to certain jobs, and travel visas. Therefore, the Citizen Score is about behavioral and social control... Were similar principles to spread in [the United States], *it would be ultimately irrelevant whether it was the state or influential companies that set the rules. In both cases, the pillars of democracy would be directly threatened.*"[41] [Emphasis added.]

The web is us, and we as a collective are it. Unfortunately, separately, and together, we have brought life to a culture that negatively affects our humanity and empathy. This cuts across the online and, through the reinforcement of such behavior, our real-life worlds. It is not realistic for anyone to opt-out of all social communities and still access what is needed to stay on the lightning bolt ride through this millennium. But increasing your awareness of the dark side of your engagement can help you balance your online and offline (real) worlds.

---

41. Source: https://www.scientificamerican.com/article/will-democracy-survive-big-data-and-artificial-intelligence/

Awareness of the Bigger Picture factors, along with heightened awareness of social platform company strategies and practices, may lead you to pause when you have choices to make. This bit of reflection will enhance your decision-making about what online information and resources you should access. It will help you make better choices.

Because the web is an organism we cannot live without, we cannot allow our online insensitivity to spill over into our real-life relationships. The Tech Giants are extraordinarily adaptive, well-managed, and essential to our lives. But they will not help us be more human except in ways that improve their profitability. We have the responsibility to retain our humanity. Yielding it without awareness is against our individual and collective best interests.

Chapter 10

U.S. Governance Fails—Covid-19

THE FIRST COVID-19 hot spot was a live animal market or biology lab in Wuhan, Hubei province in The People's Republic of China. This novel virus and associated disease were virtually invisible before the outbreak there.

Covid-19 rapidly became a phenomenon exploiting the global connectivity that has made our world smaller. It ultimately became a dark cloud over the entirety of our country and much of the world. It seriously wounded our economy and killed hundreds of thousands of Americans, more than 80 percent of them ages 60 and older.[42]

It also put an unwelcome spotlight on significant existing cracks in the foundation of our representative-based democracy.

Was there any challenge in our generation better suited for cohesive, nonpartisan, national leadership? Maybe even historic, heroic efforts? The entire spectrum of American elected officials—the President, Members of Congress, and the executive branch—kept their heads in the sand, blamed everybody but themselves, and punted their responsibilities to the states. They ghosted us at the time we needed them most.

---

42. Source: https://www.cdc.gov/coronavirus/2019-ncov/need-extra-precautions/older-adults.html

In a thoughtful essay in *The Atlantic*, "America is Having a Moral Convulsion," David Brooks wrote about Covid-19: "Americans looked to their governing institutions to keep them safe. And nearly every one of their institutions betrayed them. The president downplayed the crisis, and his administration was a daily disaster area. The Centers for Disease Control and Prevention produced faulty tests, failed to provide up-to-date data on infections and deaths, and didn't provide a trustworthy voice for a scared public..."[43]

If you are a self-interested politician, you recognize that untimely strong leadership and truth-telling can negatively affect your electability. The promises you may publicly make in the heat of a crisis may not have met voter expectations in hindsight. Staying out of sight until your next campaign may be a better course than trying to make a difference today. It is an excruciating truth, but in the context of Covid-19, this failure to lead represented a dereliction of duty. More about this and what to do about it in Chapter 34, "Radical Seniors Save the Country."

The arrival of Covid-19 exposed the differences between China's tight containment and that of most other countries. Whether the virus was introduced through contact between humans and bats or released from a lab doesn't matter. The Chinese response (if you will accept their reported number of cases and deaths) was fast, effective, and continuous.

China's current population is more than four times that of the U.S., 1,400,000,000 compared with 331,000,000. As of this writing, the number of reported Covid-19 cases in the U.S. was more than 330 times higher than those documented by China. Although we have just one-fourth of China's population, U.S. deaths were 115 times higher.

---

43. David Brooks is a contributing writer at The Atlantic and a columnist for *The New York Times*. He is the author of *The Road to Character* and *The Second Mountain: The Quest for a Moral Life*. Source: https://www.theatlantic.com/ideas/archive/2020/10/collapsing-levels-trust-are-devastating-america/616581/

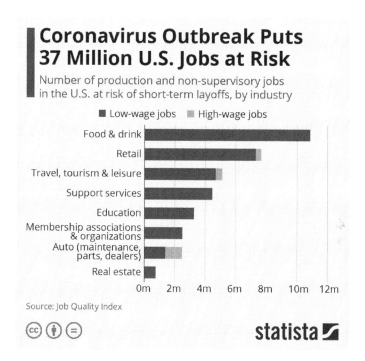

Coronavirus Outbreak Puts 37 Million U.S. Jobs at Risk

Number of production and non-supervisory jobs in the U.S. at risk of short-term layoffs, by industry

■ Low-wage jobs ■ High-wage jobs

- Food & drink
- Retail
- Travel, tourism & leisure
- Support services
- Education
- Membership associations & organizations
- Auto (maintenance, parts, dealers)
- Real estate

0m 2m 4m 6m 8m 10m 12m

Source: Job Quality Index

statista

In the aftermath of the arrival of Covid-19, I felt an unprecedented vulnerability as a citizen. A similar feeling arose from the events and consequences of 9/11, but it seemed by comparison more isolated, tangible, and contained, though devastating.

After 9/11, we rallied to search out and punish the enemy. There was a sense of belonging and pulling together. National leadership was present and accounted for and notably well-supported by the states and New York City. I felt much patriotic pride in being a part of an American people with purpose and commitment. I wore an American flag pin as a symbol of my support, and so did many others.

We saw the death toll of 2,974 lives lost from the 9/11 attack as staggering. The death toll from Covid-19 was an order of magnitude greater. During the pandemic height, we reached levels of daily Covid-19 deaths greater than the full toll of 9/11.

We have reasonably expected and trusted our national political leadership to anticipate and manage complexity and issues of scale beyond the typical capacity of individuals, select groups, and, in some cases, state governments. Examples include environmental disasters, wars, terrorists, and other threats, affecting large groups of Americans.

Upon the arrival of Covid-19 and its subsequent spread across our nation, the American people faced unprecedented uncertainty. One million or more additional Americans filed new claims for unemployment for 20 straight weeks. As many as 40 million Americans found themselves under the pressure of eviction or foreclosure.

There are many examples of missteps by our elected representatives that have landed on our heads. In just the category of fiscal management, these include deficit spending, taking on unimaginable debt, and, not least, playing political roulette with the futures of tens of millions of people reliant upon government social programs. If it isn't already, the failure to make Social Security and Medicare changes to accommodate the massive increase in aging Americans will soon be another example.

The Covid-19 pandemic opened our eyes to several startling truths about the perceived value and vulnerability of American seniors:

- Most U.S. deaths attributable to Covid-19 were of those over 60 due to this age group's vulnerability and presence of underlying chronic conditions.
- Some hospitals and other medical facilities adopted triage protocols based upon estimated remaining life expectancy. In some cases, this had the effect of depriving seniors of active, curative treatment in favor of palliative care. The latter option provides patients relief from pain and other symptoms, with the underlying cause permitted to take its course.

- Disruption in the post-Covid-19 workplace disproportionately affected middle-aged and older workers. Many of those
furloughed, laid-off, or terminated may never again attain
full-time employment. More about this in Chapter 17, "The
Financial Realities of Aging."

If the 5-, 50-, or 100-year Chinese plans included the weakening of
democratic governments, capitalist economic forms, and societies, the
purposeful introduction of a biological agent would have been a brilliant
tactic. More than the direct human and financial tolls that the pandemic extracted, it provided Chinese planners with a view of the crisis-
readiness, responsiveness, and vulnerabilities of all major countries.

America's history is replete with great victories, extraordinary results
under pressure, and at times, stellar leadership bringing our nation
together. Despite significant efforts by the emergency and medical
communities, other first responders, and many mayors and state leaders, our national response to Covid-19 was not among them.

In the future, threats may come from outside our country in the form
of terrorism, military actions, hacking of computer systems, or introducing biological agents in unanticipated ways.

There could also be internal threats, including the inflexibility and high
cost of our healthcare system, the aging out and inadequacy of the Social
Security and Medicare systems, the isolation epidemic, the disruption
in our workforce structure, and a divisive political and social culture.

The arrival of Covid-19 was a severe assault on American well-being.
The U.S. national leadership's failure made it clear to seniors that we
cannot count upon them to protect us from internal threats.

The unreliability of our government representatives and leadership has
taken its place as a Bigger Picture factor. It has created fear, anxiety,

and doubt among tens of millions of American adults. We ignore at our peril that our central government is an unstable support source.

Whether you are a senior or a younger person expecting to become one, it is better to know what you can count on and what you cannot. All generations should understand our elected national and state representatives' general ineffectiveness. It has become evident we must find solutions outside of our central government.

Fortunately, we are self-reliant and resilient people; we can do what is required. Being forewarned enables our forearming.

Chapter 11

Ecological Pain and Suffering

WE HAVE ADAPTED to significant changes over the past several decades, but there has been an enormous cost. One of the highest prices paid has been the decline of biodiversity (the variety and variability of life on Earth). We use what we want, not need, from our external environment, with highly adverse consequences.

As pointed out by Tom Friedman, we have been "...the grasshopper generation, eating through just about everything like hungry locusts..." We have been voracious consumers of credit to buy homes, second homes, swimming pools, cars, planes, vacations, electronics, and whatever our kids wanted or demanded. We have been so focused on acquiring and consuming that we have ignored many consequences of our actions.

One such outcome is the devastation wrought on non-human species. Their rate of extinction is second only to the extraordinary rise in the human population. The leading cause of plant and animal extinction is the destruction of natural habitats by human activities. Some of these include cutting down forests, wildfires, and leveling land into fields. These activities cause rapid, negative, environmental changes. Other significant causes of extinction include pollution, the introduction of invasive species (such as predators and food competitors), overhunting, and overharvesting.[44]

---

44. Source: https://en.wikipedia.org/wiki/Extinction#:~:text=Humans%20can%20cause%20extinction%20of,cause%20of%20the%20extinction%20crisis

Humans have not been up to the task of slowing the pace of extinction. Sir Peter Scott, the founder of the World Wide Fund for Nature, offered a sobering reality check, "...when we first set up WWF, our objective was to save endangered species from extinction. *But we have failed completely; we haven't managed to save a single one.* If only we had put all that money into condoms, we might have done some good."[45] (Emphasis added.)

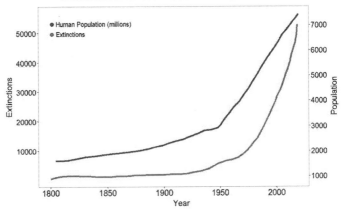

Data source: Scott, J.M. 2008. *Threats to Biological Diversity: Global, Continental, Local.* U.S. Geological Survey, Idaho Cooperative Fish and Wildlife, Research Unit, University Of Idaho.

The World Wildlife Federation's Living Planet Report estimates that just since 1970, we have lost 68 percent of all vertebrate wildlife populations: more than half of all birds, mammals, reptiles, amphibians, and fish.[46] Extinct in half a century. A million additional living species are now at risk. According to the IUCN Red List of Threatened Species, 41 percent of amphibians, 25 percent of mammals, 34 percent of conifers, 13 percent of birds, 31 percent of sharks and rays, 33 percent of reef-building corals, and 27 percent of crustaceans today are at risk of extinction.[47]

45. Source: http://archive.cosmosmagazine.com/opinion/a-plague-people/
46. Full report: https://www.zsl.org/sites/default/files/LPR%202020%20Full%20 report.pdf
47. Source: https://www.iucnredlist.org/

WWF International director general Marco Lambertini said, "… at a time when the world is reeling from [Covid-19], this year's Living Planet Report provides unequivocal and alarming evidence that nature is unraveling and that our planet is flashing red warning signs of vital natural systems failure." He continued by saying the research "…clearly outlines how humanity's increasing destruction of nature is having catastrophic impacts not only on wildlife populations but also on human health and all aspects of our lives."[48]

We are also witnessing the consequences of one action compounding others: the cascade or domino effect. There is no better example than the phenomenon of wildfires. We have seen rising air temperatures, parched landscapes, water rationing, power outages, long-term forest management failures, habitat and wildlife destruction, toxic smoke pollution, mass human evacuations, loss of homes and personal possessions, billions of animals, and many human lives. When the rains come to help extinguish fires, mudslides, flooding, toxic runoff, polluted waterways, and water supplies add to the destruction.[49]

The acreage consumed by fires in the U.S. over the past ten years is roughly equivalent to the landmass in the entire state of Colorado, the eighth largest state. An area comparable to England's size burned in the mega-blaze Australian bushfires from September 2019 to February 2020. A study by the World Wide Fund for Nature estimated that nearly three billion animals were killed or displaced.[50] More than 445 human deaths were linked to smoke from the Australian fires.[51]

---

48. Source: https://www.statista.com/chart/22845/decline-in-monitored-vertebrate-species-populations/?utm_source=Statista+Global&utm_campaign=2f70633031-All_InfographTicker_daily_COM_AM_KW37_2020_Th&utm_medium=email&utm_term=0_afecd219f5-2f70633031-299798081

49. Source: https://e360.yale.edu/features/how-wildfires-are-polluting-rivers-and-threatening-water-supplies

50. Full report file:///C:/Users/Wm%20K/Downloads/Animals%20Impacted%20Interim%20Report%2024072020%20final.pdf

51. Source: https://www.bbc.com/news/world-australia-53549936

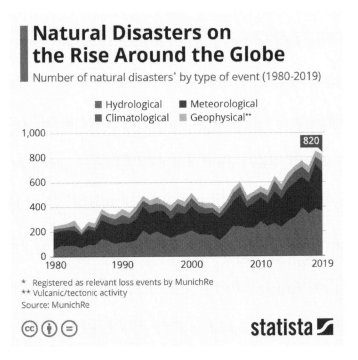

Natural Disasters on the Rise Around the Globe

Number of natural disasters* by type of event (1980-2019)

- ■ Hydrological
- ■ Meteorological
- ■ Climatological
- ■ Geophysical**

* Registered as relevant loss events by MunichRe
** Vulcanic/tectonic activity
Source: MunichRe

statista

Our collective role in creating this devastation is painful and sobering for those who can get beyond denial. It is impossible to see how we can slow our planet's destruction, let alone repair the damage already done. It cannot happen in the absence of cohesive leadership and cooperation among nations over a sustained period.

The *bigger*, bigger picture: There is an ongoing debate about the likelihood of extinction of the human species. Some say 'when,' not 'if.' The most credible scenarios have such an end attributable to the presence or creation of anthropogenic hazards. These are consequences of human action or inaction, not natural ones.[52]

Everything is connected. We are among the Bigger Picture factors. They are part of us.

---

52. Source: https://en.wikipedia.org/wiki/Human_impact_on_the_environment

PART TWO

Your Money and Your Life

Chapter 12

The Razor's Edge

LIFE ON THE razor's edge is a cold economic reality for most American households. It is even more challenging for those who have been shut or aged out of the world of work.

Most of us believe that our earning capacity will perpetually rise along with opportunities. We permit our wants to find their way onto the list of necessities. We assume that getting them now will be funded by our improving cash flow later. "My annual raise will cover the cost of the new sound system." "We can pay off the cost of the trip to Disney World out of the year-end bonus." Pretty soon, the line between requirements for living, and having what we want, is invisible. For many, the greater cash flow never comes.

The climb to significant income and wealth is always possible. However, it is unlikely you will walk on the hallowed ground of the one percent, or even the ten percent if you are not already there. It is less likely with each passing year. By the time we become seniors, most of us have learned that chasing higher income is not the answer to reaching financial equilibrium.

The daily, weekly, monthly, financial chase for many Americans is to make ends meet barely and merely. It is hoping-against-hope that you can earn a monthly income sufficient to keep most bills current.

However, a misstep can change your world. This continuous state of insecurity is like treading water—with much effort not rising, but for the moment, not sinking.

The economic predicaments that seem so unfair are often linked directly to our poor decision-making. There is no getting around it. But why do we make financial decisions against our self-interest? And why do we continue doing so?

We do what everyone around us is doing. We conform. We do it so long and well it becomes difficult to see it as the self-sabotage it is. Staying stuck in this malaise seems to provide a strange sort of reassurance. Our hand-to-mouth situation is 'normal,' no matter our income or stage of life.

When hundreds of millions of Americans accept this imbalance and the related stress and anxiety, we could chalk it up to fighting against structural or environmental issues. "The system is rigged! Nothing can be done about it. It isn't our responsibility!"

However, we have the same choice as we did with the Bigger Picture elements explored in Part One. As a starting point, we can examine these financial issues as facts. We can use them to begin improving our lives. Balance your income and expenses. It is possible to break from the herd that merely hopes for better—the one that keeps wandering in circles waiting for someone to show the way.

Chapter 13

An Affordability Crisis
and a Great Divide

THE CHALLENGES FACED by U.S. households in making expenses
match income are so pervasive that *financial fragility* has become a
way of life. Income insufficiency is the rule for many.

The challenges for senior Americans mirror those of other adults, with
several important distinctions. As a percentage of the population, there
are fewer employed older citizens. Most are living on relatively lower
and fixed incomes than when they were working. Affordability issues
are more challenging for them due to higher healthcare expenses and
other aging-related costs. The future for Social Security, a principal
income source, is often debated by Congress as something for downward adjustment or overhaul, creating income uncertainty.

Though it is difficult not to see our financial challenges as unique and
personal, this is a false belief. You will soon see that your situation is a
mirror of millions of others with slight variations. There is not much, if
anything, leftover once the bills are paid just for the necessities. Success
is when you can avoid falling behind or find you have a bit of money left
over at the end of the month (perhaps to pay more than the minimum
on your credit card balance).

Even a minor setback in keeping up the monthly cash flow could mean
the inability to borrow, loss of a go-to credit card, a lower credit rating,

a downgrade in housing, limited college choices, more challenging medical care access, deferring needed house repairs, or perhaps even bankruptcy.

These conditions are the ordinary course of living for more than 100,000,000 American adults. It is managing to carry on and hang on most of the time. Awareness of other American households' plight offers a cautionary note, even if you are fortunate to have some financial strength. It also can be a perpetual reminder to be tolerant of, if not helpful to, those having less than you do.

The American Way is one of apparent prosperity as a cover for a state of almost continuous financial anxiety. I can practically hear the chorus of, "Tell me something I don't already know." You may know it to be true in your case, but knowing it is a way of life in America may make you feel less alone. "My situation is not all that different from people with much greater resources and earning power. It turns out I am doing better than I thought." How do you feel now?

When asked to offer their view of Americans' financial situation, *95 percent of adults perceive that most Americans do not live comfortably.*[53] Almost 40 percent say they believe most meet their necessary expenses with a little left over for extras, and roughly half say they meet their essential expenses. The rest of the survey respondents believe that most Americans do not have enough money to meet basic expenses.

This sense of relative comfort differs dramatically by income group. Overall, about 30 percent of adults say they live comfortably. Forty-one percent say they meet their expenses with a little left over for extras, 22 percent say they meet necessary expenses, and seven percent indicate they cannot meet their essential expenses.

---

53. Source: https://www.pewsocialtrends.org/2019/12/11/most-americans-say-the-current-economy-is-helping-the-rich-hurting-the-poor-and-middle-class/

Most Americans do not describe themselves as 'living comfortably'

% saying they ...

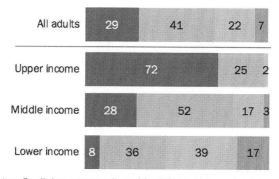

■ Live comfortably
■ Meet basic expenses with a little left over for extras
■ Just meet basic expenses
■ Don't even have enough to meet basic expenses

	Live comfortably	Meet basic expenses with a little left over	Just meet basic expenses	Don't have enough
All adults	29	41	22	7
Upper income	72	25		2
Middle income	28	52	17	3
Lower income	8	36	39	17

Notes: Family incomes are adjusted for differences in purchasing power by geographic region and for household size. Middle income is defined as two-thirds to double the median annual income for the survey sample. Lower income falls below that range, upper income falls above it.
Source: Survey of U.S. adults conducted Sept. 16-29, 2019.
"Most Americans Say the Current Economy Is Helping the Rich, Hurting the Poor and Middle Class"

PEW RESEARCH CENTER

Ironically, median American incomes have continued to rise over the past ten years and are high relative to other major countries.[54] Discomfort in America is the lap of luxury in many other parts of the world.

Unfortunately, rising American incomes have run headlong into an extended *affordability crisis*: The costs for life's necessities have continued to grow with or faster than incomes.[55] Making more money enables, at best, running in place, not advancing toward greater financial security.

---

54. Source: https://www.thebalance.com/what-is-average-income-in-usa-family-household-history-3306189
55. Source: https://www.theatlantic.com/ideas/archive/2020/02/great-affordability-crisis-breaking-america/606046/

Because yearly income can significantly vary, looking at lifetime incomes is a better way of viewing how much people earn. The real lifetime income for 90 percent of men has *decreased* over the past 50 years, despite rising incomes. According to the Bureau of Labor Statistics, this is because men's participation in the civilian labor market has been dropping steadily since 1950, when it was 86 percent.[56] It is now about 70 percent and will likely fall further in future years given the number of adults in retirement and the Covid-19 workplace disruption.

Median lifetime income for women has increased by over a third. It grew from 34 percent in 1950 to a high of 60 percent in 2000. In large part, this is due to their greater participation in the workforce. While income growth for women has been more significant, it has recently weakened and remains about 40 percent below a man's median lifetime income (when compared after age 55).[57]

Real Earnings of Men & Women
Median Earnings, full-time year-round Workers
Adjusted for inflation (CPI-U)
Source: Census Bureau   WOLFSTREET.com

Income stagnation does not appear due to a life cycle pattern of earnings but lower starting wage levels for younger generations. Young adults' prospects for lifetime earnings might be determined by age 25.

56. Source: https://www.bls.gov/opub/ted/2007/jan/wk2/art03.htm?view_full
57. Source: https://www.brookings.edu/wp-content/uploads/2018/02/es_2272018_stagnation_lifetime_incomes_guvenen_policy_proposal.pdf

In recent decades, the wealthiest 20 percent of Americans have made more significant income gains than those below them. In 2018, they made more than half of all U.S. income, with an average of $100,000 per year.

The highest-earning 20% of families made more than half of all U.S. income in 2018

Share of U.S. aggregate household income, by income quintile

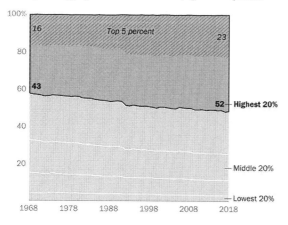

Note: Figures may not add to 100% due to rounding.
Source: U.S. Census Bureau, Income and Poverty in the U.S.: 2018, Table A-4.
PEW RESEARCH CENTER

The concentration and inequality are evident as you look more closely at the incomes of the one percent. Interestingly, the super wealthy's percentage of income is slightly higher than it was 100 years ago. It was the era of the Robber Barons. Coincidence? Take another look at the chapter on the Tech Giants. The business founders and leaders in the vanguard of the digital age may be the Robber Barons of the 21st century.

Income Concentration at the Top Has Risen Sharply Since the 1970s

Share of total before-tax income flowing to the highest income households (including capital gains), 1913-2018

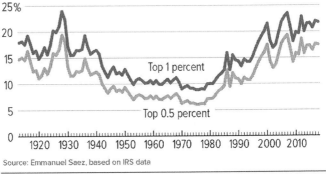

Source: Emmanuel Saez, based on IRS data

CENTER ON BUDGET AND POLICY PRIORITIES I CBPP.ORG

The income share of the one percent has risen as that of middle-income households has steadily fallen.

The gaps in income between upper-income and middle- and lower-income households are rising, and the share held by middle-income households is falling

Median household income, in 2018 dollars, and share of U.S. aggregate household income, by income tier

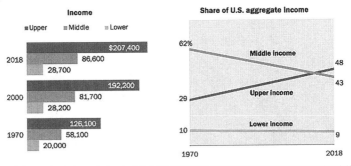

Note: Households are assigned to income tiers based on their size-adjusted income. Incomes are scaled to reflect a three-person household. Revisions to the Current Population Survey affect the comparison of income data from 2014 onwards. See Methodology for details.
Source: Pew Research Center analysis of the Current Population Survey, Annual Social and Economic Supplements (IPUMS).
"Most Americans Say There Is Too Much Economic Inequality in the U.S., but Fewer Than Half Call It a Top Priority"

PEW RESEARCH CENTER

When it comes to the measure of total *assets*, the gap is even more extreme. The top ten percent of U.S. households hold 77 percent of total assets.

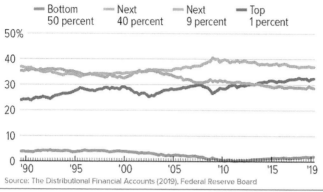

Share of Wealth Held by Wealthiest 1 Percent Has Risen Since 1989; Bottom 50 Percent Share Tiny

Share of total wealth (with groups ranked by wealth)

Source: The Distributional Financial Accounts (2019), Federal Reserve Board

CENTER ON BUDGET AND POLICY PRIORITIES I CBPP.ORG

This Federal Reserve Board chart above shows that the bottom 50 percent of households have less than two percent of total wealth. *The top one percent possess more wealth than all the middle class.*

The share of households with zero or negative net worth rose to 23 percent in 2017 from 16 percent in 2001. The bottom ten percent's real net wealth in the United States fell from negative $23,240 to negative $69,408 between 1999 and 2017.[58]

The irony of the extraordinary effort to keep our noses above the financial water line is that we view income as among the lesser valued measures of successful living. The factors that align with people's success definition continue to favor relationships, health, and lifestyle over material things, career, and wealth. The top six attributes of success in living include:

1.   (Tie) Spending quality time with family.
2.   (Tie) Being healthy.

---

58. Source: https://www.mckinsey.com/~/media/McKinsey/Industries/Public%20 and%20Social%20Sector/Our%20Insights/The%20social%20contract%20in%20 the%2021st%20century/MGI-The-social-contract-in-the-21st-century-Full-report-final.pdf

3. Having a good relationship with your spouse or partner.
4. Being financially prepared for the future.
5. Having good work/life balance.
6. Being a good parent.

Each of these elements overshadowed things like "Earning a high income" (No. 12), "Owning the home of your dreams" (No. 11), and "Having nice belongings" (No. 19).[59]

Historically, these latter attributes have been considered gateways to the American dream, and their pursuit has taken large chunks of our lives. Perhaps we should look at what people do, not what they say.

---

59. Source: https://news.northwesternmutual.com/planning-and-progress-2019

Chapter 14

Seeking Balance: Having and Being

THE BALANCING ACT during the remainder of your life expectancy could be between 'having' and 'being.' *Having* is the sufficiency of necessities and material possessions. *Being* is about personal development, individual expression, life experiences, and associations with others.

Americans believe that acquiring the bare necessities should not require struggling. These essentials are food, water, clothing, shelter, sanitation, heat, access to medical care, love, and affection. This grouping includes a few things excluded from the typical definition of what is required to rise above the poverty threshold. But I believe these elements are what most American citizens would view as fundamental living requirements.

Having is easily definable, and the acquisition of necessities is a powerful master. Because of the immediate consequences, *having* requires our attention for most of our lives. We tend to focus on the *fear of insufficiency*—of not having what we need.

We readily get on a commuter train five days a week for 30 years or wake up at 5 a.m. to go to a job that we could do with our eyes closed. The pursuit of *having* can lead to a numbing and vacant life.

Once material needs are covered, American adults typically seek to acquire possessions that reflect their view of what they *should* possess. They decide what to do with their discretionary income if any. Extra resources can result from working or be acquired through borrowing. The latter is a tried-and-true pathway to living beyond your means (at least for a while).

We may need even more money to get to the next level of our American dream. This status could have been self-determined or defined for us by an endless tidal wave of marketing images, noise, and calculated persuasion.

In the pursuit of *having*, you may feel measured against the amorphous standard of the success or failure of those around you. You may deem yourself a failure if you do not have x, y, and z. When you possess those, you may consider yourself a failure if you cannot get XX, YY, and ZZ. Consumption beyond our means is almost irresistible, and the goalposts keep moving.

Nobody told us that *having* in America is a lifetime pyramid scheme that you are welcome to play until all your money is gone or your earthly time has expired. The opportunities for richness in life are diminishing moment-by-moment along with the sand in your life's hourglass.

At a gut level, most of us know that our survival is not in question. Taking care of the *having* does not have to be an exercise in perpetual penance. You do not have to strap yourself to the *having* process to the exclusion of all else.

No matter the rationale, if you have done this to your detriment, choose to forgive yourself for being swept up. Get on with doing what you can to change your lifestyle in your best financial interest.

You will see families and individuals around you that seem to make space and time for life experiences in the present. Many do it no matter their degree of *having*. Owning a private jet ready to take you to an exotic destination for a picnic on a secluded beach might enhance your life. Or you could walk with your family to a neighborhood beach for a picnic. These experiences have more to do with the people around you than the mode of transportation.

Please begin thinking about what adequacy or sufficiency could be for you in the case of necessities. What would you be willing to sacrifice? What commitments would you be ready to make? In Chapter 20, "How to Relieve Financial Anxiety Starting Right Now," we will lay the foundation for you to do what is required to make it happen.

Chapter 15

Financial Anxiety:
An American Condition

FOUR FINANCIAL TRUTHS relating to the current American adult population are representative of the status of tens of millions of Americans.[60] These facts do not fully reflect the economic devastation wrought as a function of the Covid-19 pandemic. When fully known, more tens of millions could find themselves in a more tenuous financial state, and those already there, further pushed to the brink.

Over 100,000,000 adult American employees
are living paycheck-to-paycheck

A CareerBuilder survey found that those employees saying they live from paycheck-to-paycheck could be as high as 74 percent.[61]

Having a higher salary does not mean that money challenges evaporate. Nearly ten percent of workers making $100,000 or more indicate they usually or always live paycheck-to-paycheck. Almost 60 percent of people at that income level also are in debt.

---

60. Source: U.S. Census Bureau data The adult population is 256,000,000 (out of an estimated total U.S. population of 330,000,000+). The difference of 74,000,000 is the population under the age of 18.

61. Source: http://press.careerbuilder.com/2017-08-24-Living-Paycheck-to-Paycheck-is-a-Way-of-Life-for-Majority-of-U-S-Workers-According-to-New-CareerBuilder-Survey

Twenty-eight percent of workers making $50,000 to $99,999 usually or always live paycheck-to-paycheck, and seventy percent are in debt.

Half of those making less than $50,000 usually or always live paycheck-to-paycheck.

According to Nielsen Global Consumer Insights, 57 percent of workers indicate they could not live off savings if they did not work for *a single month*.[62]

Over 200,000,000 American adults have savings of less than $5,000

A recent survey found that 80 percent of American adults have less than $5,000 in their savings accounts. Over 115,000,000 respondents (45 percent) indicate they have *no savings*. This survey was completed before the economic consequences of Covid-19 began to unfold in 2020.[63]

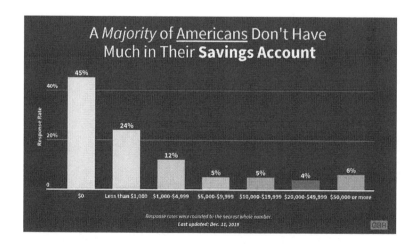

62. Source:https://www.nielsen.com/us/en/insights/article/2015/saving-spending-and-living-paycheck-to-paycheck-in-america/

63. Source: https://finance.yahoo.com/news/survey-69-americans-less-1-171927256. html, https://www.gobankingrates.com/saving-money/savings-advice/americans-have-less-than-1000-in-savings/?utm_campaign=901519&utm_source=yahoo.com&utm_content=12

The Federal Reserve Board said in its July 2020 report, "...while financial planners often recommend having a liquid savings cushion of at least three months of expenses, we find that about 60 percent of [American] families do not satisfy this rule of thumb, including most married families with children, and many high-income families."

When asked to include all cash, bank accounts, investments, and retirement accounts at their disposal, 35 percent of Americans say they have less than $1,000 in savings, 22 percent say they have less than $200. When looking only at retirement saving across all generations, there is little difference.

American adults owe an average of $92,727 in total consumer debt.

This debt includes credit card balances, student loans, mortgages, and more.[64] The average American household with a credit card carried $8,398 in credit card debt.[65] Sixty-one percent of American consumers have at least one credit card, and the average person with a credit card has four of them.[66]

Approximately nine percent of all credit card balances in the United States were 90 days or more delinquent before the economic impact of job losses and savings depletion associated with Covid-19.[67]

Among Americans who carry debt (157 million Americans have credit card debt and 44 million have student loan debt outstanding), a third of their monthly income goes toward paying it off, exclusive of mortgages.[68]

---

64. Source: https://www.bankrate.com/personal-finance/debt/average-american-debt/#:~:text=As%20of%20November%202020%2C%20consumer,student%20loans%2C%20mortgages%20and%20more.

65. Source: https://www.debt.org/faqs/americans-in-debt/

66. Source: https://www.experian.com/blogs/ask-experian/consumer-credit-review/

67. Source: https://www.fool.com/the-ascent/research/credit-card-debt-statistics/ from the Federal Reserve Board, the Consumer Financial Protection Bureau, and Experian.

68. Source: https://news.northwesternmutual.com/planning-and-progress-2020

Digging deeper into the credit card debt numbers, the Northwestern Mutual Planning & Progress Study found:

- Nearly one-third of Americans are paying interest rates above 15 percent on their credit cards
- Close to one-fifth did not know their interest rate, with Millennials most likely not to know (22 percent).
- Twelve percent expect to be in credit card debt between 11 and 20 years, and seven percent expect their credit card debt to last more than 20 years.
- Ten percent say they "always" pay only the minimum payment.
- Of the 42 percent of Americans who report holding credit card debt, over half the money (52 percent) went toward paying for necessities like rent, utilities, and groceries.
- On a positive note, the study found that a quarter of Americans report having no debt.

Over 150,000,000 adult Americans regularly face major unexpected expenses and are challenged to cover them.

Unexpected expenses come up so frequently that they should be a budget line-item. You know what they are: an emergency room visit, new tires, a roof leak above your bed, the deductible on your car insurance, unplanned travel to see an ill parent or child, the cost of medication not covered by insurance, and on-and-on.

Over 70 percent of U.S. adults regularly face unexpected (but unsurprising) expenses. Transportation issues (25 percent), housing repairs/ maintenance (23 percent), medical care for an injury or illness (21 percent), and inability to keep up with debt (20 percent) are at the top of the list.

Recently, a sizeable share of adults appeared to be better able to handle a small financial emergency. Among all adults, the share who reported they would pay an unexpected $400 emergency expense entirely using cash, savings, or a credit card paid off at the next statement, increased to 70 percent.[69] The other 30% would have to borrow the money, sell something, or could not come up with it at all. Be reminded that 30 percent of the American adult population is about 75,000,000 people.

Just as with income, savings, and consumer debt, being cash and asset poor is more typical than not. Fifty to 80 percent of adults face the same plight—slightly better or worse financial challenges—as do you. This predicament is evident in the level of concern about financial matters reported across the American adult population.

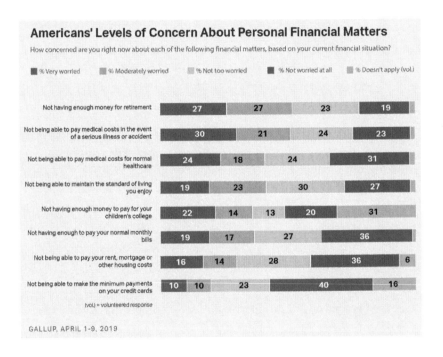

Americans' Levels of Concern About Personal Financial Matters

How concerned are you right now about each of the following financial matters, based on your current financial situation?

■ % Very worried   ■ % Moderately worried   ■ % Not too worried   ■ % Not worried at all   ■ % Doesn't apply (vol.)

	% Very worried	% Moderately worried	% Not too worried	% Not worried at all	% Doesn't apply
Not having enough money for retirement	27	27	23	19	
Not being able to pay medical costs in the event of a serious illness or accident	30	21	24	23	
Not being able to pay medical costs for normal healthcare	24	18	24	31	
Not being able to maintain the standard of living you enjoy	19	23	30	27	
Not having enough money to pay for your children's college	22	14	13	20	31
Not having enough to pay your normal monthly bills	19	17	27	36	
Not being able to pay your rent, mortgage or other housing costs	16	14	28	36	6
Not being able to make the minimum payments on your credit cards	10	10	23	40	16

(vol.) = volunteered response

GALLUP, APRIL 1-9, 2019

The Willis Towers Watson Global Benefits Attitudes Survey measured the attitudes of over 40,000 employees at medium and large private sector companies. A total of 8,000 U.S. workers participated in the survey.

---

69. Source: https://www.federalreserve.gov/publications/2020-update-economic-well-being-of-us-households-overall-financial-security.htm

This survey is notable because it includes people receiving regular cash flow. The findings tie together many of the points highlighted above.

The Global Benefits Attitudes Survey found:

- Thirty-eight percent of workers live paycheck-to-paycheck.
- Thirty-nine percent could not come up with $3,000 if an unexpected need arose within the next month.
- Eighteen percent of employees making more than $100,000 per year live paycheck-to-paycheck.
- Seventy percent are saving less for retirement than they think they should.
- Thirty-two percent have financial problems that negatively affect their lives.
- Sixty-four percent believe their generation is likely to be much worse off in retirement than their parents.

Many adult Americans across all generations face this reality daily: juggling fixed or reduced incomes in the face of an unrelenting stream of bills and rising costs for necessities. This pressure has grown due to cash flow pressure from many sources: job losses, higher housing, healthcare and transportation costs, savings depletion, and the overhang of existing debt.

Constant financial anxiety and worry have become the norm for a large percentage of Americans. Months and years of our lifetime allocation of days pass quickly in the numbness of financial futility.

It does not have to be this way. Relieving this psychological cloud can become your priority right now. Untethered aging includes loosening the financial knots that we have permitted to tie us down. I will show you how to accomplish this, one step at a time. My prescription represents a potential solution for you or someone you know needing this kind of breakthrough.

Chapter 16

The Misfortune of the Junior-Seniors

THE ECONOMIC CONSEQUENCES set in motion by Covid-19 rapidly and dramatically changed the world of work as we had known it. Many businesses were required to assess urgently: the value of brick-and-mortar offices, maintaining company headquarters in densely populated, high-tax, high cost-of-living locations, commuting, business travel, face-to-face meetings, and many other existing paradigms. Digital video and other technologies were quickly adopted and integrated to fill the void left due to working remotely. These tools enabled a rapid move to home offices.

Big retailers got bigger, and many smaller ones went out of business or on life support. For the sake of safety and convenience, customers rapidly moved to online shopping and direct-to-home order fulfillment. Shoppers made fewer trips outside their homes. When they did, it was to the acre-sized, consolidated shopping towns such as Walmart, Costco, Target, Home Depot, Lowes, and others.

In the face of an avalanche of chaotic, forced change, we collectively created a new form of order. We quickly learned to get along without restaurants, movie theaters, in-person church services, haircuts, and leisure travel.

Many households suddenly had no income. In the immediate aftermath of the arrival of Covid-19, nearly 40 million jobs disappeared or were left unfilled. Former workers of all ages began seeking new employment, flex jobs, or freelance work in the gig economy. The demand for employment swamped the supply.

Seemingly overnight, people in their fifties and sixties found themselves confronted with income, affordability, savings, and debt challenges similar to those of older Americans. You might call them the new 'junior-seniors.'

Smart, experienced, displaced former executives, managers, and other skilled workers found themselves chasing fewer opportunities and dollars. Hourly workers in the retail, hospitality, and transportation sectors were sidelined, with no viable work in view.

Prior mass avoidance of STEM education (science, technology, engineering, and math) by Boomers and the following American generations made this worse. There are many well-paying jobs available in these categories. As a percentage, fewer Americans qualify for them due to the absence of education, experience, and a continuing lack of interest.

The junior-seniors typically have twenty-five years or more remaining in their life expectancies, but their employment and other income prospects have dimmed. The income expected to fund or add to retirement accounts over the next ten to fifteen years is unlikely to be available.

Complicating circumstances for them is that Social Security benefits will have to wait until they are 67 (or older if Congress raises the qualifying age in the interim). This income deferral places them in a more difficult position than seniors already having reached retirement age. Many in this new junior-senior category will not have money to add contributions to Social Security. Therefore, their benefits will be lower when they qualify.

These are among the reasons I include all adults 55+ in the category of seniors. The only distinction in many cases is the additional number of years during which junior-seniors may face income challenges.

If you are in the gap between an exit from the workforce and receiving Social Security (or know someone who is), achieving a balance between expenses, income, and other resources, has become necessary and, in fact, urgent.

Chapter 17

The Financial Realities of Aging

THE LIFESTYLE PROJECTED by many seniors was unrealistic and almost certainly would not have played out as hoped, even before the arrival of Covid-19. In many cases, retirement resources were inadequate from the start compared with requirements. Downward pressure on Social Security income, the inability to stay in or get back into the workforce, higher health care costs, the early onset of chronic diseases, and many other factors represent significant retirement headwinds.

We will not know the full economic consequences of Covid-19 on seniors (and the junior-seniors) for a long time. There doesn't appear to be light at the end of the tunnel. Financial fragility has become a normal state-of-being for millions of seniors. This status has slowly but persistently led to significant personal challenges and stress for people accustomed to being self-reliant. If you are feeling it, you are far from alone.

Many American seniors indicate they are on solid financial ground today yet have mixed feelings about their prospects. Almost 25 percent are not confident their income will be sufficient to meet monthly expenses over the next five to 10 years. It is not at all clear that conditions will improve during that period. How will 95+ million people ages 55 and over cover their necessities for an additional five, 10, or even 20 years on the income and other resources available to them?

Social Security Income

For most seniors, a principal 'paycheck' is a monthly check or bank deposit from the Social Security Administration (SSA). About 97 percent of the total population aged 60 to 89 do now or will receive Social Security benefits based upon the qualifying requirements.[70]

A Social Security check is more modest than many people realize. The average SSA retirement benefit recently was $1,514 a month, or about $18,168 a year.[71] Couples in which both parties qualified for benefits received $30,991 a year.

At the time of this writing, 52.5 million Americans are age 65 and older. SSA provides over 50 percent of income for about half of them and 90 percent or more for almost a quarter.[72] Half of all seniors have less than $25,600 in yearly income from all sources.

The poverty guideline for individuals (defined by the U.S Department of Health and Human Services) is $12,760 yearly. In the U.S., for a family of four, the poverty line is $26,200 a year.[73] This guideline is based on the Census Bureau's information and is updated by evaluating recent price changes using the Consumer Price Index.

Without SSA benefits, about 40 percent of Americans ages 65 and older would have incomes below the poverty line, all else being equal.[74] With SSA payments, about ten percent of Americans over the age of 65 have income below the poverty line. The anti-poverty effect has been more significant for African Americans: nineteen percent live in poverty,

---

70. Source: http://www.ssa.gov/retirementpolicy/fact-sheets/never-beneficiaries.html
71. Source: https://www.ssa.gov/OACT/ProgData/icp.html
72. Source: https://www.ssa.gov/policy/docs/ssb/v77n2/v77n2p1.html#:~:text=We%20find%20that%20about%20half,percent%20of%20their%20family%20income.
73. Source: https://aspe.hhs.gov/poverty-guidelines
74. Source: https://www.cbpp.org/research/social-security/social-security-lifts-more-americans-above-poverty-than-any-other-program

but 52 percent would have done so had they not received SSA payments. For Hispanics, the numbers were 17 percent and 46 percent.

Social Security Dramatically Cuts Poverty Among Seniors

Percentage of seniors in poverty, 2018

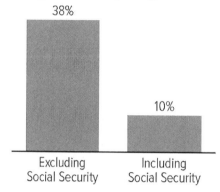

Source: CBPP, based on data from the Census Bureau Current Population Survey, March 2019.

CENTER ON BUDGET AND POLICY PRIORITIES | CBPP.ORG

More than half of those in the lowest 20 percent of recipients received all their income from SSA. For those receiving SSA income alone, affording rent, food, and other basic needs is a significant challenge as SSA covers less than half the average costs of living.[75]

The value of SSA benefits has fallen during the past decade and is likely to decline further.[76] I believe the official retirement age will continue to rise.[77] Lengthening life expectancies, fewer full-time workers making

75. Source: https://aspe.hhs.gov/poverty-guidelines
76. Source: https://www.nytimes.com/2019/12/14/business/retirement-social-security-recession.html?utm_campaign=Economic%20Studies&utm_source=hs_email&utm_medium=email&utm_content=81962356
77. Source: Changes enacted in 1983 have pushed up the program's qualifying age—that is, the age when claiming gets you 100 percent of your earned benefit. It is increasing to 67 for workers born in 1960 and later. https://www.ssa.gov/news/press/factsheets/basicfact-alt.pdf

contributions, regular outlays to tens of millions of people today, and the rising population of those over 65, will drive an upward adjustment, perhaps to age 70 or more eventually. I also believe that more people aged 55 to 65 will make earlier moves into the retired ranks due to the changing workforce dynamics. New retirees more than doubled from 2019 to 2020—an indication of what is to come.

The pressure on Social Security will continue to increase over the next couple of decades, as shown in the chart below.

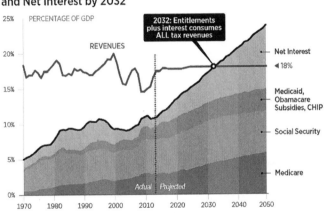

All Tax Revenue Will Go Toward Health Care, Social Security, and Net Interest by 2032

Something will have to give. It is too early to know if it will be the commitments to seniors and the disadvantaged in our society. According to the latest government data, the SSA started drawing down its assets to pay retirees all their current benefits. Unless there is a creative political solution, SSA trust funds could be depleted by about 2035.[78]

Seniors' best interests will require a resolution for SSA well in advance. For this and many other reasons, seniors will need to engage in political

---

78. Source: https://www.nytimes.com/2019/06/12/business/social-security-shortfall-2020.html

activism. In Chapter 34, "Radical Seniors Save the Country," I will explain why there is no choice.

Work

Earning money from employment can represent a supplement to retirement income. Sixty-five percent of Americans ages age 55 through 64 still participate in the civilian labor force. For those ages 65 through 74, the participation rate falls to 28 percent, and over 75, to nine percent. I expect these participation rates to plummet due to the workforce disruption tied to Covid-19.

This reality will continue to sting older employed workers and those unemployed but expecting to return to work. Nearly three million older workers left the labor force in the immediate economic aftermath of Covid-19. According to a New School Retirement Equity Lab report, over half of older unemployed workers now face involuntary retirement.[79]

If you are over 65 and out of the workforce, you will unlikely make it back. As mentioned, many junior-seniors will face the same fate, just earlier.

There is another monstrous workforce disruption affecting all American workers. Automation of labor-intensive businesses has been rising for a long time but accelerated in the wake of Covid-19. *Forty-three percent of companies now expect to reduce their workforces because of new technology, including artificial intelligence.*[80] The World Economic Forum estimates that *40 percent of workers will need to develop new skills* to qualify for emerging job categories. These facts are game-changing for seniors counting on income from working to cover some portion of their necessities.

---

79. Source: https://www.economicpolicyresearch.org/images/INET_docs/Status_of_older_workers_reports/Q1_2020_OWAG_V12.pdf
80. Source: https://www.weforum.org/reports/the-future-of-jobs-report-2020/digest

Given these trends, senior workers' participation in the workforce will decline from current levels. In part, this will be due to the challenges of retraining, competition from younger workers, and age discrimination in the selection process for retraining and hiring. *Good paying work for seniors is heading toward extinction.* Please assume that you must change your lifestyle and reduce your expenses.

If you decide to work full-time until you die, you can certainly try. It may be necessary, or it may be that pursuing a higher level of *having* is the way you feel alive and fulfilled. Working may have become the default choice over your lifetime, one that you cannot or do not want to give up.

In any event, if you are willing to take on the associated challenges, working represents a direct way to increase your income in retirement. No matter your willingness to work, staying in or re-entering the workforce is more uncertain and challenging than ever.

Other Income

The following information is among the conclusions of a survey conducted by *Kiplinger's Personal Finance* in partnership with the Alliance for Lifetime Income. Many of today's seniors have income from sources aside from SSA and working, including:

- A retirement savings plan: 66 percent
- A pension from an employer: 50 percent
- Interest income from CDs and savings accounts: 39 percent
- Income from bonds, dividend-paying stocks, or REITs: 33 percent
- Annuity income: 21 percent
- Rental income from real estate: 11 percent
- Income from a trust: 5 percent
- Other: 6 percent

Confidence is mixed among those receiving 'other income' that their total income will be sufficient to live comfortably in retirement:

- Very confident: 25 percent
- Somewhat confident: 48 percent
- Neither confident nor unconfident: 17 percent
- Somewhat unconfident: 8 percent
- Very unconfident: 3 percent

Nearly three-quarters of respondents are very or somewhat confident that they can create a secure income stream in retirement. About half of pre-retirees and 70 percent of retirees surveyed receive a pension or its equivalent. Women, respondents in their fifties, and those with a net worth of under $500,000 are less confident about achieving a secure retirement.

Some of the concerns cited relating to the sufficiency of cash flow and the challenges of affordability are:

- Inability to afford long-term care—65 percent
- Running out of money—58 percent
- Inability to afford quality health care—55 percent
- Not enjoying retirement—53 percent
- Not having enough money to live comfortably—53 percent
- Not being able to travel as much as desired—45 percent
- Not getting a regular paycheck—39 percent
- Not being able to find new activities—29 percent
- Leaving a job (not by choice)—28 percent
- Having to rely on adult children for financial support—23 percent

Income insufficiency and affordability challenges in our country represent a source of lifetime worry for seniors and other Americans of all ages.

Savings and Debt

Some research indicates the number of seniors with savings of less than $25,000 is near 50 percent. With 50+ million Americans over the age of 65, this amounts to roughly 27 million seniors with insufficient savings to help pay for essential expenses. These conclusions exclude the new category of junior-seniors created as a function of the Covid-19-related shifts in the world of work.

Almost a quarter of seniors do not have a financial savings plan for their retirement years. This reality, however, crosses all generational cohorts. "The first thing to know is that the average American [of any age] has nothing saved for retirement or so little it won't help. *By far, the most common retirement account has nothing in it*," according to TheStreet.com.[81] [Emphasis added.] Sources differ, but the story remains the same. Northwestern Mutual's study concluded that 21 percent of Americans have no retirement savings and an additional ten percent have less than $5,000.[82] This 30% of adult Americans represents over 77 million people.

As reported by the National Council on Aging, 60 percent of households headed by an adult aged 65 or older (with any debt) had median consumer debt of $31,300.[83] The Federal Reserve Board found that seniors' median debt grew by over 400 percent between 1989 and 2016.[84] Electing to take on more debt ahead of or during retirement is choosing to perform a high-wire act with no net.

---

81. Source:https://www.thestreet.com/retirement/average-retirement-savings-14881067

82. Source: https://news.northwesternmutual.com/2018-05-08-1-In-3-Americans-Have-Less-Than-5-000-In-Retirement-Savings

83. Source: https://www.ncoa.org/economic-security/money-management/debt/senior-debt-facts/

84. Source: https://repository.upenn.edu/cgi/viewcontent.cgi?article=1531&context=prc_papers

An 'obvious truth' is that most seniors have lower and fixed incomes, modest savings, more significant health care issues and costs, and only a small percentage earn income from work.

Expenses

We spend a working lifetime believing that the promised land of financial sufficiency is higher income. It is, however, only one of the variables and has its limits. The other principal variable is managing the expense side of the equation. Expense adjustments can be achieved with more certainty than increasing income, especially after a one-way move out of the workforce.

Following is a breakdown of the largest average annual expenses among older households, according to data from the Employee Benefit Research Institute:

Spending Category	Age 50 – 64	Age 65 – 74	Age 75+
Housing	45.9%	44.9%	45.6%
Food	11.0%	11.2%	11.2%
Health Care	7.8%	9.6%	10.6%
Transportation	13.9%	12.0%	9.7%
Entertainment	10.2%	10.5%	8.3%
Gifts, contributions	4.7%	5.4%	6.3%
Clothing	2.9%	2.9%	2.7%

Here is a bit more detail. The Health and Retirement Study (HRS) and the Consumption and Activities Mail Survey (CAMS) examined the spending behavior of older Americans in the 50 to 64, 65 to 74, and 75-and-older age groups.[85] Following are some of the findings:

---

85. Source: https://www.ebri.org/retirement/publications/issue-briefs/content/how-do-retirees-spending-patterns-change-over-time

- Total average annual spending is lower for households in the older age groups.
- Housing is the largest spending category for every age group.
- On average, the older age groups spent less on food, clothing, and transportation.
- The average amount spent on entertainment declined by age.
- The share of health care costs in households' budgets increased with age. However, the average annual portion of health costs for the 65 to 74 and 75-and-older age groups declined after 2007 (the year after Medicare Part D went into effect).
- A larger share of income was spent on housing and food by low-income households across all age groups.

Here is a chart that more clearly shows the spending shifts across ages:

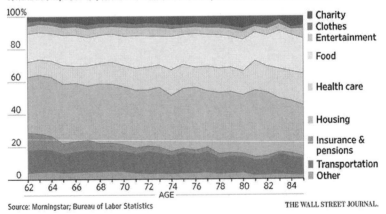

How Spending in Retirement Changes Over Time
The relative amount spent on insurance and pensions, which includes premiums and contributions, declines, while the relative amount spent on health care increases.

Source: Morningstar; Bureau of Labor Statistics   THE WALL STREET JOURNAL.

If you have not regularly lived within your means over the past 20, 30, or 50 years, why would you believe that more income could now be the answer? If you are now 65, assume you will live to 85. Also, consider that your existing resources will take you through the next ten years at your current spending rate. When those have passed, you will be out of resources for the next ten. Would you bet on your ability to work after age 75 to cover your needs during your remaining life expectancy? I hope not.

The way to greater ease in living at any age is in your perception of what is required. *Adequacy and sufficiency* represent the new comfort zone for living. Who knew that income meeting expenses would be a psychological and philosophical journey?! I assure you that it is, and we have just scratched the surface.

Unexpected Expenses

Almost 200,000,000 adult Americans regularly face unanticipated major expenses or financial setbacks and are challenged to cover them if they can. The average American spends about $7,429 more than budgeted each year.[86] In addition to those faced by other adults, seniors have more significant healthcare and other age-related expenses.[87]

The probability of overspending income and other resources by seniors is often related to catastrophic medical expenses. For instance, of those who spent 20 percent or more of their income on medical costs, 85 percent of them experienced a budget deficit. By comparison, of those who spent five percent or less of their income on health-related costs, only 20 percent experienced a shortage.[88]

Suffering perpetual financial anxiety is no way to live. Closing the gap between your income and other resources and your expenses can change your life. How you got into your current position no longer

86. Source: https://www.fool.com/retirement/2019/10/11/the-average-american-overspends-by-nearly-7500-per.aspx
87. Source: https://www.fool.com/retirement/2020/01/24/5-unexpected-expenses-that-could-derail-your-retir.aspx
88. Source: https://www.ebri.org/retirement/publications/issue-briefs/content/spending-patterns-of-older-households

matters. As I pointed out earlier, assigning emotional value to dollars and cents simply slows your progress in changing the status quo.

The best way to get started is by understanding the facts of your financial situation in the context of your probable remaining years of living. Open your eyes and begin doing what is required. The cavalry is not coming.

Chapter 18

Releasing the Retirement Fantasy

OVER ONE-QUARTER of adults consider themselves retired. Nearly half retired before age 62, and a quarter between 62 and 64.[89] A desire to do things other than work, or spend more time with family, are the most common reasons for retiring. Forty percent of those retiring before age 62 and 30 percent of those ages 62 through 64 indicated that poor health contributed to their decision.

More than 20 percent of those retiring before age 65 said the lack of available work contributed to their decision. This latter category will significantly rise in the economic wake of Covid-19, including many junior-seniors forced into early exits from the workforce.

Allianz Life Insurance Company of North America sponsored a study entitled *Reclaiming the Future.* It focused on seniors' expectations for retirement. Ninety-two percent of the respondents believe there is a retirement crisis in America.[90] Their perception is rooted in the lack of preparedness. More than a third of the respondents agreed with the statement, "Financially speaking—I feel totally unprepared for retirement."

89. Source: The Fed—Retirement. https://www.federalreserve.gov/publications/2019-economic-well-being-of-us-households-in-2018-retirement.htm

90. Source: https://www.allianzlife.com/-/media/files/allianz/documents/ent_991_n.pdf?la=en&hash=22B9CE8151AB813C34696723818B40C4AF46D62D

Over half of the respondents say they fear not covering their expenses. The daily grind and financial worry that were hallmarks of working life, for most, will continue into retirement.

Complicating this is that longer life expectancies require paying for essentials for many more years. To the question posed in the Northwestern Mutual survey, "What do you fear the most: outliving your money in retirement or death?" sixty-one percent said they were less fearful of dying. *Among those in their late 40s and married with dependents, the number afraid of outliving their assets rose to 82 percent.*[91]

Another question posed in the Allianz Life survey was, "Is it more likely that you will be struck by lightning or get your full due from Social Security?" Almost 40 percent responded that they believed it more likely that they would be hit by lightning than be paid under the terms of their original agreement with Social Security. Among moderate-income respondents, more than half agreed. For the record, the likelihood of being struck by lightning in your lifetime is about one in 15,300.[92]

The referenced Allianz Life survey was completed in 2010, just after the Great Recession's primary waves had passed and well before the arrival of Covid-19. If anything, there is a more dismal view today.

However, there are two seeds of hope in reaching retirement age. First, if you are in this group, you are among the living. Between 13 and 20 percent of Americans die before age 65.[93] Second, if you have an annual household income of *less than* $37,300, you are in the top 70 percent of surviving seniors.[94]

91. Source: https://news.northwesternmutual.com/planning-and-progress-2019
92. Source: https://www.weather.gov/safety/lightning-odds
93. Source: https://data.worldbank.org/indicator/SP.DYN.TO65.MA.ZS?locations=US
94. Source: https://www.aei.org/carpe-diem/explaining-us-income-inequality-by-household-demographics-2018-update/

Most seniors adapt to lower and fixed incomes. They make their way with Social Security and other non-work, non-savings, income sources. For the most part, they adjust their living expenses downward, even though they were unwilling to do so for most of their lives.

Although there are many options, inertia or forces we view as beyond our control can keep us from cutting our housing expenses. We may never embrace the possibility of taking on a voluntary two-year program to pay off credit card debt. Living with less anxiety and more freedom later means taking proactive actions now to align expenses and income.

Spending can find its equal in income even at the extreme. People with incomes at the lowest levels in our society survive by accessing and acquiring the necessities. Even with our challenges, Americans' lives are abundant compared with those faced by many others in the Earth's human population.[95]

Over one billion people around the world live on less than $2.50 per day. If you raise daily income to $10.00, the number increases to over four billion, more than half of the global population.[96] Over 800 million people worldwide do not have enough food to eat. More than three million children die from malnutrition each year. Nearly a billion people live without electricity. Forty million children live without adequate shelter. More than 750 million people lack sufficient access to clean water. There are 270 million children with no access to health services, and 1.7 billion people do not have a bank account or access to essential financial services.

---

95. Source: https://finca.org/campaign/world-poverty/?gclid=CjwKCAiAnIT9BRA mEiwANaoE1Yvepo6xzmIui-8BrHF7hYbRtLVYCgTiMcRDkdVokMi82fFbmuVFQxoC RekQAvD_BwE

96. The daily income for an individual living at the poverty threshold in the U.S. is about $35.

I intend to offer a sense of reality *and* empathy, though it isn't easy to convey a voice tone in writing. Even in America, there is significant hardship in surviving on low incomes challenged by a growing crisis in affordability.

No matter the specific numbers in your case, nor what category on any survey your circumstances may represent, the answer is reframing your perception of what a life of well-being means. First and foremost, one of the pillars of well-being at any age is not permitting your expenses to exceed your income. You can free yourself from many of the bonds of financial insufficiency by achieving that balance.

In the upcoming chapter, "How to Relieve Financial Anxiety Starting Right Now," I will explain a process through which you may reconcile your income, expenses, and lifestyle choices.

Chapter 19

There is No Problem without a Solution

FOR MOST OF our adult years, those who may not have had our best interests in mind have been insisting on grabbing our attention. Over the past 20 years, the tsunami of technological developments bombarded us with a cacophony of noise and impressions. Social media platform companies are monopolizing our attention. We have persevered on the monotonous treadmills of work. These external requirements and distractions have taken attention away from tending to our financial well-being.

We have viewed the portrait of the average American household's financial status both before and after retirement. You do not have to go far to meet adults dealing with all the challenges described. Just look around the room, no matter if it is a fancy ballroom or a corner restaurant. Maybe even your living room.

Most Americans run faster today to enable spending more for the same or a slightly better version of bare necessities. If we are not yet there, it will not be long before many more households in America are considered financially fragile. You might already be in this status if you are living paycheck-to-paycheck, carrying consumer debt more than 25 percent of your annual household income, and unable to save even a modest percentage of your income.

Consider the charts and graphs I have shown you as reminders that you are not alone. Seeing them should affirm that your situation is simply part of the American way of life. Knowing these facts may open the way to conversation with your co-workers, neighbors, and children about the pervasive reality of these challenges.

With the waves of economic, world-of-work, savings depletion, and other consequences of Covid-19, these life challenges have landed heavily on seniors' heads. Tens of millions of Americans *under 65*, including many younger adults, have not been spared either. By the time the Baby Boomers hit a median age of 35, their generation had owned 21 percent of the nation's wealth.[97] Last year, Millennials—a cohort that will soon reach an average age of 35—owned just 3.2 percent of total wealth.

Intergenerational wealth

Share of national wealth owned by each generation, by median cohort age

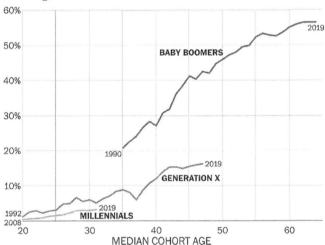

Source: Federal Reserve Distributional Accounts   THE WASHINGTON POST
Chart adapted from Gray Kimbrough

---

97. Source: https://www.washingtonpost.com/business/2019/12/03/precariousness-modern-young-adulthood-one-chart/

You might say, "You don't understand. My situation is unique. I have more pressure than everyone else to provide for my family. It would be irresponsible of me not to worry nor allow myself to feel this pressure." Maybe you would say once more, to bolster your false courage, "I thrive under pressure!" But I have proven that your situation is not unique and what you feel is a symptom of a widespread American condition. So, how can you lighten the load of financial worry?

Recall the quotation, "Insanity is doing the same thing over and over and expecting different results." If the attention you have given to reducing this pain over the past months or years has not changed your results, why not try something different?

Reframing the perpetual effort to earn and pay, earn, pay, borrow, earn, pay, and pay, into acceptance that this is the way of our lives in America, can be a relief. But even more liberating could be changing your lifestyle to be in sync with your income and resources. I offer you a process you can start right now to reduce the weight of financial insufficiency that has burdened you most of your life.

Chapter 20

How to Relieve Financial Anxiety Starting Right Now

FORCES BEYOND YOUR control can take everything you possess except your freedom to choose how you will respond. If we can extract most of the emotion from our view of any problem, it becomes easier to develop actionable solutions. A problem is not inherently "bad," "good," or "embarrassing," and living is not the absence of challenges; it is overcoming them.

Ninety-two percent of U.S. adults agree that nothing makes them happier or more confident in life than when their finances are in order. Despite this link between financial stability and emotional well-being, most Americans have not crossed the gap to act.

A Northwestern Mutual study[98] found that *monthly,*

- Forty-five percent of Americans say debt makes them feel anxious.
- Thirty-five percent report feeling guilty about the debt they carry.
- Twenty percent report that debt makes them feel physically ill.

---

98. Source: https://news.northwesternmutual.com/2019-09-17-U-S-Adults-Hold-An-Average-Of-29-800-In-Personal-Debt-Exclusive-Of-Mortgages and https://news.northwesternmutual.com/planning-and-progress-2020

- Thirty percent say financial anxiety causes them to feel depressed.
- Twenty percent say debt impacts their relationship with a partner or spouse
- Twenty percent indicate that debt affects their job performance.

Most of us could add a phrase of explanation to each of these expressions: *"…because I choose to accept my situation and can't or won't take action to change it."*

We have proven to ourselves over and over that fear has virtually no value in changing the outcomes of the problems to which they are attached. Worry about finances will not change our circumstances enough to matter.

Worrying focuses your attention on the problem, not the solution. It represents a continuous negative affirmation. "I have a problem." "I have a problem." "I have a problem." How much time and attention should that mantra be permitted to take up in your life? You can focus on actions once you recognize that the problem also contains the seed of a solution.

I have lived through most of the challenges highlighted in the past several chapters. As I reached 70, I considered the trade-offs of continuing to work versus making changes to reduce my expenses. I asked myself, "Do you want the measure of your life to be the stuff that you have when you die? How much of your remaining lifespan are you willing to spend on the effort?" I decided to live within my current means and made it my top priority.

Some of my decisions and actions included moving to a new state with a lower cost of living and tax rates, renting an apartment rather than buying a house, significantly reducing my furniture and household items, and buying what I needed at consignment stores. I packed up clothes for donation, jettisoned most of what used to be called memorabilia (it was never viewed and took up a lot of room), and began eating at home most of the time. I eliminated a pay-over-time federal tax liability early and paid off all other debt.

It didn't happen overnight. This process was a sustained effort over almost two years. But once I recognized that a downshift in my lifestyle was an accommodation worthy of the pain, I stayed on course. I made it a creative process to find workable solutions, but I wasn't seeking perfection.

The bottom line is that arriving at a place where my income and financial resources met my expenses has freed me from most worry about the subject. Coincidentally (probably not), I am happier than I have been for most of my life. I am confident that if I need to adjust my lifestyle further, I can do it. An incredible gift of freedom was within my grasp, just overcome by being outer- and other-directed most of my life.

Focus on Financial Wellness

Worry about money matters is woven into our lives as though part of our DNA. We feel pressure on many financial fronts while mainly accepting the lot. We avoid taking even small steps in the direction of our individual economic best interests. Yet, as Americans, we also have a long history of adaptability through chaotic and complex challenges.

Nearly all Americans admit they are not making time to prepare for the future financially. *Ninety-seven percent of American adults indicate that they make no time.*[99] About half of them say they want to do

---

99. Source: https://www.fool.com/the-ascent/research/average-american-time-personal-finance/#:~:text=Onlypercent203percent25percent20ofpercent20American spercent20spend,thanpercent20theypercent20didpercent20inpercent202016

something, but only three percent take any action on household financial matters an average day. Those that do—do it in a hurry.

On average, Americans spend fewer than three minutes a day managing their household finances. Those who make this brief effort spend an average of one-minute forty-eight seconds per day for financial management and 36 seconds using professional and banking services.

By contrast, the average American spends over 2.3 hours per day watching traditional television.[100] What are we thinking?!

What if you committed just 30 minutes of each day to understand, plan, budget, evaluate, improve your financial literacy, and retool your approach to personal and household financial matters? Could you spare 30 minutes a day to work on the problem that may weigh heaviest on you?

Could you cut your social media, streaming, gaming, or television time by 30 minutes a day? If ten percent of those aged 55 and older would do this and stick with it, 9.5 million people could be free of some or all the bondage of financial worries.

The overarching objective for such a daily 30-minute financial wellness session (your "Financial Focus") is to answer this question: "How will I live within my means for the rest of my life?" Let's call it the *Big Question*. If you knew that committing 30 minutes a day to answering it could change your life for the better, could you do it? I mean, *commit* to it, not try.

Make a Financial Focus appointment with yourself and put it on your calendar. Turn off your phone and leave it in another room. Find a quiet

100. Source: https://www.statista.com/statistics/186833/average-television-use-per-person-in-the-us-since-2002/#:~:text=Estimates%20suggest%20that%20in%20 2020,minutes%20watching%20TV%20each%20day

place and do your best to sit with these issues at the same time each day. Dedicate this time; do not be distracted by other people or things.

During those 30 minutes, you will assemble and review the facts relating to your income, assets, spending, savings, debts, and the other elements of your overall economic situation. You will explore the potential solutions that could create a shift in some or all these elements. You will also use the time to learn more about budgeting and for becoming literate in basic financial matters.

Remember that you are working to create actions that can lead to answering the Big Question, "How will I live within my means for the rest of my life?"

Your first level of commitment is to do this for 30 days. If seven days a week does not suit your daily rhythm, take the weekends off. Permit yourself to reduce your dedicated time to 30 minutes, five days a week. By the end of a month, you will have dedicated ten hours of attention to solving what could be the most problematic issue in your life.

During those first hours of dedicated attention, the facts can be gathered, absorbed, and considered. It is a beginning. It is an order of magnitude greater focus than most people give when carrying around the same or more significant burdens.

The Sentence Completion Tool

Nathaniel Branden, a clinical psychologist, author, and the godfather of the self-esteem movement, used a sentence completion exercise with his patients.[101] He described it this way: "The essence of the sentence completion procedure is to start with an incomplete sentence, a 'sentence

---

101. Sentence Completion II: Nathaniel Branden. http://www.nathanielbranden.com/sentence-completion-ii

stem,' and add different endings. The sole requirement is that each ending is a grammatical completion of the sentence." Write at least six endings for each stem and complete each in two or three minutes.

A short response time is part of the design for accessing what you *already* know and believe. What comes up for you from top-of-mind? The responses are your 'grist for the mill'—the pieces for creating an actionable answer to the Big Question.

I based the following approach on Dr. Branden's sentence completion exercise. During the first two weeks, complete six different endings for the sentence stems below on the day indicated. As Dr. Branden said, "Empty your mind of expectations concerning what will happen or what is 'supposed' to happen. Do not impose any demands on the situation. Do the exercise and move on…"

Complete each one as quickly as possible. Do not censor yourself or edit the results. You already possess many of the answers. You will be tapping into what you already know but may not be able to see clearly. If you overthink it or second-guess yourself, you will sabotage your efforts. If you draw a blank, invent an ending. Just get something down on paper.

- Day One:
  - I could bring greater awareness to the financial challenges in my life…
  - Increasing my income…
  - Taking full responsibility for my financial condition…
  - If I don't take personal responsibility for my financial well-being…

- Day Two:
  - Living within my income…
  - Reducing my expenses…
  - If I bring 5 percent more awareness to my spending…

- If I bring 10 percent more awareness to avoiding/reducing my debt...

- Day Three:
  - I could reduce my housing expenses...
  - I could reduce my transportation expenses...
  - I could reduce my food expenses...
  - I could reduce my medical expenses...

- Day Four:
  - I could embrace changing my lifestyle...
  - Realistically managing my income and expenses requires...
  - I could pay down my credit card debt in full...
  - A viable housing alternative...

- Day Five:
  - I could reduce my total expenses by 20 percent within 90 days...
  - I could eliminate my financial worries within two years...
  - I am resisting making changes in my financial best interest...
  - If I needed help in answering the Big Question...

After you finish completing the sentences for the day, put them away and don't look at them again until after you address the others. Wait a full day before addressing the next sentence stems. Do not worry if you create similar or redundant endings. This exercise is about using the power of a time constraint. Please simply act on this approach rather than worrying about whether you are doing it right.

Over the weekend following your first five days of effort, review and reflect on your completed sentences. After you do so, address the following sentence stem (with six different endings, please): "If what I wrote this week is true, it might be helpful..."

During the second week, *repeat the work of the first week*. Follow the same process and don't reference your earlier work. Don't worry about redundancy—it doesn't matter. The objective is to get the words down on paper for your later review. New thoughts will come up for you— write them down as they do. At the end of the second week, again create six endings to complete the following sentence stem, "If what I wrote this week is true, it might be helpful..."

The sentences you have completed over your first ten days of attention contain the initial actions you can take to cut expenses, reduce debt, and relieve your mind. They were there all the time. From the completed sentences, outline and prioritize the actions to be taken and add a due date for each. The latter creates a self-imposed deadline, another constraint to keep you in action. Put the steps and the due dates on your calendar. Once per week, complete this sentence stem with six different endings: "If I stop this Financial Focus process, the consequences..." Select a day and time each week to do this.

Have you been worrying about personal financial issues on and off for three years, 20, or all your adult lifetime? Why not commit a minimum of 30 minutes a day to a Financial Focus session for one year? You will have dedicated the equivalent of three and a half 40-hour weeks to the task by the end of it. You will discover immediate actions you can take to change the status quo. It may involve income opportunities but more likely shifting your lifestyle to reduce expenses. This approach is a sure path to reducing the worry that may have dominated your consciousness for a long time.

Reducing Expenses is Essential and Doable

Based upon an analysis of data from Earnest Research by *The New York Times*, the chart below provides a vivid snapshot of the impact of the Covid-19 virus on the economy and Americans' immediate financial response.[102] It tracked and analyzed the credit and debit card purchases of nearly six million people in the United States during the last 12 days of March 2020.

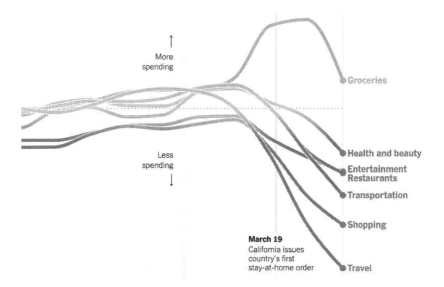

California issued the first stay-at-home order on March 19, 2020. Other than stockpiling groceries, credit and debit purchases had started falling. A week later, thirty states still did not have stay-at-home orders in place, but spending continued to decline rapidly. It took less than two weeks for Americans to make 25 to 75 percent cuts in the specified spending categories.

Due to the issuance of U.S. government stimulus checks, the availability of more information about the potential course of the Covid-19 pandemic, and the lifting of some of the stay-at-home orders, spending recovered.[103] Two months later, spending had rebounded but was still well below pre-Covid-19 levels when compared with the prior year.

102. Source: https://www.nytimes.com/interactive/2020/04/11/business/economy/coronavirus-us-economy-spending.html
103. Source: https://www.statista.com/chart/22091/change-in-consumer-spending-due-to-coronavirus/

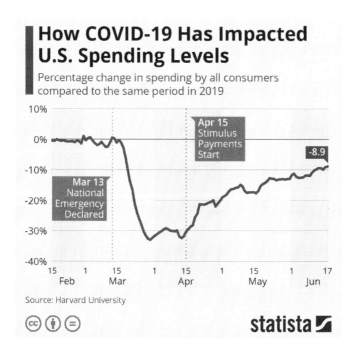

How COVID-19 Has Impacted U.S. Spending Levels

Percentage change in spending by all consumers compared to the same period in 2019

Apr 15 Stimulus Payments Start

-8.9

Mar 13 National Emergency Declared

Source: Harvard University

statista

The specter of the unknowns relating to Covid-19 stimulated a high level of motivation for taking immediate actions. Although the circumstances were unique, the response was a powerful illustration of urgently accomplishing what previously would have seemed impossible.

When surveyed six months later, three-quarters of U.S. adults had made financial adjustments. Nearly 40 percent had cut their monthly expenses from pre-Covid-19 levels, while about 25% were putting off major financial decisions. Interestingly, another quarter reported increasing contributions to their emergency/retirement savings or other savings or investments.[104]

We knew what to do already. We possessed the answers for rapidly reducing our expenses. We needed the inspiration to act with urgency, and we got it. We took action in our best interest without procrastinating.

---

104. Source: https://www.nefe.org/research/polls/2020/covid-19-survey-update.aspx

Could you foresee your annual expenses exceeding your income for the rest of your life? Is this uncertainty any less critical than the personal economic threats evident in the immediate aftermath of Covid-19's arrival? Envision yourself at age 80, unable to pay your heating bill or the co-pay for a prescription. Would you want to avoid that possibility? What could you do to create the motivation to take actions that are as responsive as those to an external threat?

Tens of millions of Americans made significant lifestyle changes within two weeks and continued doing so for months. Through your Financial Focus, you will discover realistic actions you can take to help you resolve the Big Question. Even if it takes a year or longer, you can do what is required.

I once led a small but thriving software company, an early entrant to the peer-to-peer networking technology space. Microsoft became interested in our approach. It would have been less painful if Microsoft had offered to buy our company, but instead, they hired our best two software engineers. It quickly became apparent that our small company could not fund what was sure to be extended litigation with Microsoft over the matter.

The software solution that was our reason for existing showed up as a feature in the next version of Windows. It was included free with virtually all new personal computers. Our product quickly became difficult to sell at any price.

We aggressively cut costs as our revenue declined. We made a significant effort to keep as many people employed for as long as possible. We spared nothing in the effort to keep our company alive. As the CEO, I finally said to our board, "The fat is gone, and the lean is gone. There is nothing more to cut."

One of our board members, Kathy (Braun) Lewis, was an executive at Western Digital. They competed in digital storage, one of the most price-sensitive computer hardware sectors. I remember to this day what she said to me in no uncertain terms, "There is *always* more that can be done to reduce expenses. But you must do more than chopping. It requires seeing and doing things that you couldn't have before sawing into the bones." I left out the expletives that conveyed her passion, but she was right. I have never forgotten it.

You can use this approach to reduce household expenses. It is a matter of cutting where possible but also requires different thinking. In the case of the above-referenced company, part of the reinvention was through acquiring two small businesses. They became part of the new core. The company survived its reincarnation and lives today, 25 years later.

What are your actual needs now, not five years ago? Could they be accommodated in new ways? What could be modified or substituted? What do you now care about most and least? What if you stopped caring what other people thought?

Completing the Financial Focus sentence stems should be a 'what if' creative exercise, not a forced march. Take your time and allow yourself some leeway with the answers. There may be the seed of something useful, even in the absurd ones. You can't predict the next source of inspiration. Deciding, committing, and taking the actions will require some pain. The presence of 'good pain' means you are on your way to changing your circumstances.

The Distinction Tool

A distinction is a difference between two or more things or the recognition of such a difference. For our purposes, I prefer this more activist version, "A distinction is a difference that you have noticed or decided is important. Often used to separate relevant things from all others."

You will create distinctions by isolating the things relevant to improving your financial situation from all the other noise. In discovering what is required to live within your means, you must decide what is essential for you to see, know, and use. You will find an immediate difference between necessary knowledge and everything else.

You have done this repeatedly but may not have identified it as creating distinctions. Recall a circumstance where you felt transported to a state of highly selective awareness. Think of an emergency where you could only see, hear, and recall from your memory the stuff that would help you deal with it. You found the information captured in your 'distinction filter' brought new and actionable information precisely, rapidly, and continuously.

Consider the games kids play when traveling. Find the numbers from one to 100; find yellow things; find things beginning with the letters in the alphabet, and so on. They instantaneously could see an incredible richness of what was needed to take the next step. The tool of distinction helped them quickly locate what was required. Without creating a distinction by setting the game parameters, the objects needed for advancing the game would remain an invisible part of the passing landscape.

Here is another example. As I was formulating the concept for, researching, and writing this book, I found myself distinguishing things even potentially related to it from everything else. I would see, hear, and observe things related to the Bigger Picture factors, aging, the American financial dilemma, and much more in news reports, conversations, and other information sources. I might even see something of value in email spam or junk mail. Even if I wanted to ignore these inputs, I could not.

Your raised level of consciousness for identifying the things that might help you is almost magical. Consider distinction to be a version of the law of attraction—it brings what you need or want.

You can turn this powerful tool into conscious, proactive use for completing the sentence stem, "I can live within my means for the rest of my life…" The more precise you can be in crafting what is required to change your game—the rest of the sentence—the more pronounced the separation of those things will be from all others. You will possess what is needed to advance the process of improving your financial situation.

The corollary to the commitment of 30 minutes a day for your Financial Focus is this: Give up thinking, worrying, stressing, and all other connections with the financial matters in your life for the rest of your waking hours. You have little to lose and a lot of potential time to gain. If you work eight hours a day and add thirty minutes for your Financial Focus, you still have eight or more hours for pursuits free of your previously persistent financial hangover.

By the end of the year, you will have discovered and made some adjustments to improve your economic condition for the better. If not, you may conclude that your situation is what it is. You will have proven for yet another year that you can keep yourself and your family afloat by doing what you have always done. Over a few years, you may continue proving that you can make ends meet without borrowing. You do it uphill, downhill, and against the wind. You do it through economic upturns, downturns, and uncertainty.

If you are not working or have reduced working hours, financial concerns will loom larger. You can and should dedicate more time each day to discovering and acting upon what is needed to shift your financial status quo. Consider it a job, a requirement in your life. Still, though, dedicate the time rather than permitting it to be a constant hovering presence. It is more efficient, and you must create a life beyond such worries. There is living to do even in the face of financial challenges.

Some seniors will experience changes in their ability to make financial decisions as they age. A NEFE grant study at the University of Alabama at Birmingham identified early declines in financial skills among cog-nitively normal aging adults.[105]

Some of these skill deficiencies include taking longer to complete finan-cial tasks, missing key details in financial documents, having trouble with everyday math, a decreased understanding of financial concepts, and more difficulty identifying risks in investment opportunities. If this becomes the case, you can arrange for a trusted family member, friend, or a reliable financial advisor in your community to assist.

I understand that there are adults for whom this Financial Focus pre-scription will sound hollow or false. Poverty and adverse living condi-tions are present in this country that a commitment to Financial Focus or reframing of perspectives cannot address.

Financial insufficiency for some is a function of the longstanding repression of significant minorities and groups in our country. This economic status can be the result of systematic exclusion from educa-tion, work, and other opportunities. Social and economic program-matic solutions must be extended, created, and implemented to reach appropriate and lasting outcomes. These issues and solutions are be-yond the scope of this book.

By confronting your financial challenges through a daily Financial Focus, you will learn more about solving other difficult problems. You will gain more through your confrontation of reality than by accepting the status quo. If you want your situation to change, you must think and act differently. If you choose to do nothing to shift the imbalance in your finances, it is proof that the fear associated with creating a way out of it owns *you*. Turn it around. Own *it*.

---

105. Source: https://www.nefe.org/research/research-projects/completed-research/2016/early-warning-signs-of-impaired-financial-skills.aspx

Chapter 21

The Meaning of Commitment

YOUR FINANCIAL FOCUS must be a *commitment* to yourself and those who depend upon you. A commitment is doing what is necessary to accomplish a specific objective or fulfill a promise, particularly one of high value.

Commitments will consume a relatively larger portion of your mental and energetic resources, so only a few can be managed at a time. A commitment should be reserved for occasions when you must—absolutely without fail—accomplish the goal to which it is attached.

An *intention* does not rise to the level of a commitment. One example is your annual list of New Year's resolutions. Most of us understand that those are statements of what we *might* do. You can readily abandon an intention. A lapse related to it may not even register with you; it just fades away.

Commitments, once made, must be renewed daily. This revival is an energetic infusion to shape, improve, or modify what must be done. It permits us to pursue the most important interests in our lives and never be bored with or overwhelmed by the process.

Once made, periodically ask yourself, "Is my approach to this commitment continuing to serve my interests? Have I learned or accomplished things that require adjustments?" These questions and the answers to them are vital to achieving your goals.

Hurdles, challenges, resistance, and avoidance inevitably arise, no matter the level of our commitments. It would not be life if they didn't. Substantive transformation is rarely quick and painless; it happens over time.

There is wisdom in this excerpt from George Leonard's *Mastery: The Keys to Success and Long-Term Fulfillment*: "Backsliding is a universal experience. Every one of us resists significant change, no matter whether it's for the worse or the better... it doesn't necessarily mean you're sick or crazy or lazy or that you've made a bad decision in embarking on the journey of mastery. In fact, you might take these signals as an indication that your life is definitely changing—just what you've wanted... *Be willing to negotiate with your resistance to change.*"[106] [Emphasis added.]

Commitment is evident during an emergency or similar crisis. You will find yourself urgently driving prioritization, energy, decision-making, and action. If you characterize your commitments to yourself and others as necessary solutions to an *ongoing crisis*, you will have infused them with the energy needed to take action every day.

Consider lacking an answer to the Big Question as a crisis. Is knowing how or whether you might be able to live within your means for the rest of your life, not an urgent matter?

The personal power you call upon in a crisis, or another matter of urgency, is an extraordinary willingness and ability to be creative and innovative. When you combine a commitment with urgency, the change you desire will inevitably occur.

---

106. Source: https://www.amazon.com/Mastery-Keys-Success-Long-Term-Fulfillment/dp/0452267560/ref=tmm_pap_swatch_0?_encoding=UTF8&qid=16122 03694&sr=8-2

Any of us might profess a commitment that declines in vigor. It may morph into something we examine from afar or pursue in fits and starts. Your commitment is evaporating if this is your choice for too many days in a row.

It will have descended to the level of something in which you may have an interest but is no longer a priority. Somewhere along the way, it ceased to have the consistent urgency that is the true hallmark of commitment. It has instead become an *option*, something one *might* or *might not* do. It has lost the required energy.

Although Americans are known for their pioneering spirit and willingness to accept difficult challenges, we identify as risk-averse. The findings from Northwestern Mutual's 2019 Planning & Progress Study suggest that when U.S. adults face choices about how much risk to take, most prefer to play it safe.[107] Nearly three-quarters reported being more comfortable reducing risk to ensure the safety and stability of their savings and investments, even if it means the potential for lower returns.

The study also found that the average American's financial risk tolerance (defined as their comfort level with taking financial risks to seek financial returns) is 4.9 out of 10 (with one being 'very conservative' and ten being 'very aggressive'). Considerably more people fall on the risk-averse end of the scale, with 30 percent in the one to three low tolerance range versus 14 percent between eight and ten.

If you look back to the point that 97 percent of Americans spend no time preparing for their financial future, isn't this neglect the epitome of bold risk-taking rather than risk-aversion? Inaction can be as much or more of a risk than taking action. Yet tens of millions of Americans do nothing when it comes to financial self-interest. Again, what are we thinking?!

---

107. Source: https://news.northwesternmutual.com/planning-and-progress-2019

We readily assume risks across spending, borrowing, saving, and preservation of lifestyle without examination. This is hardly risk-averse behavior. As we have seen, what we say in response to surveys and what we do in practice can differ significantly.

Having a legitimate answer to the Big Question is a way for those 55+ to lessen future financial hardship. The risks associated with not addressing it rise every day. Doing something about it becomes less likely as time passes. Procrastination can be numbing, self-defeating, and rob you of choices.

The biggest motivator should be your desire to live, now and for the rest of your natural life, *without the sword of financial uncertainty suspended over your head.* Please do not let another day pass. When the chips are down, and you are ready for your reality to be different than it is, your life can change in a moment of choice, coupled with an ongoing commitment. There is no risk in embracing a 30-minute Financial Focus and no downside. Not only is that a good bet—it is worthy of your commitment.

Chapter 22

Silver Linings

HARDSHIP IN LIVING in America has been a palpable condition for some, for decades. Some Americans, including Blacks, Hispanics, the undereducated, and to some extent women, have been hardened by dedicating most of their time scrambling to acquire the mere necessities. This challenge has been invisible or ignored by most Americans not experiencing it.

These pressures became even more significant in the context of the economic tumult brought about by Covid-19. Its impact on American institutions, economics, and our social fabric, was harsh in a nation that, for the most part, has been free of these kinds of wounds. The impact disproportionately affected those already fighting to keep their heads above water.

The only redeeming feature, and it is difficult to say it let alone view it as such, is that dealing with *continuing* hardship may feel less brutal than confronting it for the first time. Many Americans have bit-by-bit discovered what it means to feel continuous financial pressure.

Covid-19 may just have been a catalyst exacerbating conditions of decline long in the making. But it felt as though a massive shift occurred with no warning. The term perfect storm applies to the situations confronted by many middle and lower-income Americans with the arrival of Covid-19. Many otherwise responsible individuals had been living beyond their means for decades. Overconsumption and debt had become a way of life.

The population explosion of the past 50 years now manifests as a caravan of seniors: Over 10,000 more citizens move through the age 65 gateway each day. They are confronting different and much more challenging economic and social conditions than expected. These trials coincide with a time in life when there are fewer options and safety nets and more vulnerability.

I believe there are silver linings in an understanding of the facts about widespread financial insufficiency. There is a legitimate opportunity to hit the reset button on one of our most significant psychological stressors. One path to creating financial freedom (or get as close as realistically possible) for your last chapter of living is to take the actions required to ensure your expenses do not exceed your income and assets. If you haven't taken these steps before now, it is most assuredly not too late. And now is a far sight better than later.

The resulting lifestyle may be different than what you expected, hoped, or to which you had become accustomed or feel entitled. It could be better than you thought or be such that you feel regret for not having done more to prepare.

Without achieving a state of financial equilibrium, you may, always and unnecessarily, wake up each day with a pervading sense of fear and anxiety.

As mentioned above, one of the most startling of many surprising financial revelations was this one, "Nearly all Americans [97 percent] admit they are not making time to prepare for the future financially."[108]

---

108. Source: https://www.fool.com/the-ascent/research/average-american-time-personal-finance/#:~:text=Only%203%25%20of%20Americans%20spend,than%20they%20did%20in%202016.

It seems improbable that you are a maverick if you DO make time and progress in seeking freedom from your financial shackles. Strangely, it is outlying behavior today.

One of the most famous of all Baby Boomers was Steve Jobs, co-founder of Apple, one of the Tech Giants. He was the force behind the development and presentation of a television ad that ran, just once, during the Super Bowl held in January 1997. It celebrated the change-makers.

> "Here's to the crazy ones. The misfits. The rebels. The trouble-makers. The round pegs in the square holes. The ones who see things differently. They're not fond of rules. And they have no respect for the status quo. You can quote them, disagree with them, glorify or vilify them. About the only thing you can't do is ignore them. Because they change things. They push the human race forward."

The definition of a senior radical today simply could be, "I am getting my financial house in order!" Do it. Be a wild and crazy household budget balancer, and then help others do it. "Here's to the crazy ones. The misfits. The rebels..." and "The financially responsible."

Freedom, generally, is having the ability to act or change without constraint. Something is "free" if it can easily change and not be kept in its present state. It is associated with having free will and the absence of undue or unjust restrictions.[109]

To achieve financial freedom, you must create an actionable answer to the question, "How will I live within my means for the rest of my life?" You now have one possible approach to start immediately. Commit to engaging in a Financial Focus session for 30 minutes, five days a week. It is a beginning that requires little time and effort but has a high potential for changing your life for the better. It may even set you free.

---

109. Source: Wikipedia. https://en.wikipedia.org/wiki/Freedom

Chapter 23

Choosing Creation

SENIORS CANNOT IGNORE the Bigger Picture factors nor financial realities and challenges. You know too much. The intention for beating the drum about these points was to provide a context for weighting your priorities for the home stretch of your life expectancy.

The ultimate question in your quest is, "Will you create or react?" Creating represents proactivity in building a life rich in experiences during your senior years. Reacting accepts the status quo without challenge or through yielding to others' choices.

Choosing creation is an expression of ownership of your choices and consequences and an openness to reinvention. It doesn't matter what you may have said or done before. If you choose it, your future can represent a blank canvas.

These terms, creator and reactor, are not mere labels. In his book, *Creator,* Steve Chandler brought the dichotomy of these behavioral and attitudinal choices to a level of distinction. Simply put, there are two types of people in this world: creators and reactors. He wrote,

> When things get challenging, we complain and react. We have learned that from all of the people around us all our lives. Therefore, it's not surprising that we don't access creativity in the face

of a new situation. Any new twist or turn in the blow of life and we respond like reactors: "Well *this* sucks."

Creators are people courageously allowing their true nature to shine through and create. And the reactors merely people who were obsessed over the obstacles to their awareness (known as beliefs) of who they really were.

You can continue to be a part of that victim energy for the rest of your life if you want to. Or you can create. The choice is always yours.

He describes an encounter with his friend and mentor, Steve Hardison, that underscores what creators (and owners) do:

He used to ask me two questions, over and over in the course of our work together. When I described a problematic situation in my life, he would listen carefully and then say, "Okay, given that that's the situation [the obvious truth], what would you like to create?"

Notice that it was not, "How do you want to solve it?" As if the problem had all the power. As if the problem was a bomb, we had to carefully disarm… He always saw creativity as having all the power. And together we didn't really have to 'solve' anything… What we created made the problems fade from all relevance.

And the second question was.

"Who do you need to be [to be that creator]?" Because he always knew, and I learned through practice, that I could create that being. I could create who I needed to be.

If you are a creator, you are an owner of the process for solving your problems. If you are a reactor, you are a victim of the process. Potential positive outcomes will be ignored or rejected as being too hard or for some other excuse. A reactor (victim) will rarely own the failure. You will again hear, "It wasn't my fault." or "I can't."

The time is now to understand that in your world—the rapid, complex, perplexing, and uncertain place—the answers required for a fulfilling life are not outside you. They are within you and your grasp. The outside is always pulling, begging, and insisting that the answers are there—but they are not. Your assessment, understanding, and ability to create, are the only things you need to trust.

We live in a world full of sounds and images of exaggeration, falseness, and fakery. Why would you trust any of that external noise more than your voice?

American psychologist Albert Ellis wrote, "The best years of your life are the ones in which you decide your problems are your own. You do not blame them on your mother, the ecology, or the president. You realize that you control your own destiny." In your senior years, you might discover that it is your choice to show up as the courageous catalyst for your own change.

> "No one can build you the bridge on which you, and only you, must cross the river of life. There may be countless trails and bridges and demigods who would gladly carry you across, but only at the price of pawning and forgoing yourself. There is one path in the world that none can walk but you. Where does it lead? Don't ask, walk!" —FREIDRICH NIETZSCHE

Do you perceive this kind of shift as beyond you because you are not employed, do not have connections, money, status, recognition, or because you think you do not deserve it? I suggest that if this is your self-concept today, it is the very reason to choose the high road of self-reliance.

The assessments that will provide an answer to the question, "How will I live within my means for the rest of my life?" will not be perfect. But isn't it better to discover a *good* solution sooner than waiting for the elusive *perfect* one?

Conditions and circumstances will change based upon your first, active decisions. You will gather more inputs and information from them, enabling you to make course corrections as needed. These adjustments will move you closer to clarity yielding better decisions.

It is time for you to determine and acknowledge the choices that are in your best interest in the days, months, and years ahead. These decisions that you cannot yield to others. The freedom you can find by creating an answer to the Big Question will rightfully be yours. This psychological declaration of independence is something that is not up for a vote. As you create a new context for living and act on it, the results will be yours alone.

If you have spent all or a part of your lifetime-to-date caring, and maybe even worrying, about other's assessments of you, it is time to reject them. How many people will notice or care that as a person of 67, 74, or 82, you make decisions that are different than 30, 20, or 10 years ago? Two people, 20, 50? I would say too few to mention and none who matter. Only you will take your last breath. Who cares if someone not living in your skin and circumstances judges you? It is trivial when compared with the inevitable approach of the end of your earthly life.

Honesty must be the foundation for recasting your financial situation to deal with fewer resources and a longer lifespan. Wishing that the facts will move in your favor if you 'give it time' is false hope. In the quiet reflection of your daily Financial Focus, the only mind working on the answers to the Big Question is yours. Nobody else can call you out if you are uncommitted or denying reality. Nobody but you will have to live with the consequences. Tell yourself the truth as you can best determine it, and frequently confirm it.

Never apologize for the condition of your finances or your lifestyle. It is what it is, and you own it. Saying, "I am sorry for you to see that my lifestyle is not what you thought," is unacceptable. It is apologizing for being you. It is unimportant what other people think, and you owe no explanation.

Financial sufficiency should be considered a lifetime challenge to be managed and coped with, but not obsessed over. If you thoughtfully but urgently create a path to financial adequacy for your necessities, you can live the rest of your life with little concern for the material. You can break from the prison of need and scarcity to the freedom of seeking purpose and meaning, the subjects of Part Three. The richness of your life will be a function of the future choices you make, starting now. They are not about material possessions. They are about seeing and believing in yourself as a self-reliant senior American.

Ironically, the biggest hurdle to firmly owning the rest of your life is embracing another obvious truth: Your strength is in the uniqueness you already possess. Personal power lives in your differences, your authentic self. We repeatedly deny our value in being just as we are. But that incarnation has gotten you through to where you are today. During your senior passage, you being *you*, yet more essentially so, will move you in the direction of personal freedom.

PART THREE

Carpe Vitam (Seize Life)

Chapter 24

The Value in Reframing

LEAVING FEAR BEHIND is always just one question away. What might it be? Perhaps this: "*What if I brought the same courage and commitment in creating my life thus far to the taking of a single, bold step into what's next?*" From that new perspective, we can see things differently, and when ready, take a second step. With a movement or two away from our status quo, we can get into the always accessible realm of reinvention. Or, as established in the last chapter, into the process of creation.

Many of us are psychologically unprepared for the road ahead. The upheaval and challenges described in Parts One and Two require rational new perspectives and significantly improved coping skills. Attempting to move forward with an inefficient trial-and-error approach and perhaps while looking backward is more likely to keep us in place.

The Bigger Picture factors and others beyond our control or even influence have contributed to a rising sense of powerlessness. The generations *under* age 55 are challenged by the same unease but appear through no fault of their own to have even greater susceptibility. This vulnerability has gradually grown into one of those difficult to define, non-specific ailments. It is there and real but defies a description.

Many of us seniors must plan to meet our living requirements for 10, 20, or 30 additional years. The journey for most has become too long and challenging to attempt alone. We will require something more than self-reliance alone to cope successfully. In the next chapter, we will review these individual requirements as a foundation for the introduction of *social self-reliance,* a source of external support for personal well-being.

A well-known quotation attributed to Charles Darwin offered, "It is not the strongest of the species that survives, nor the most intelligent that survives. It is the one that is *most adaptable to change.*"[110] [Emphasis added.] We must embrace change through rapid adaptation. This skill will ensure that we can meet our needs as long as necessary.

Over the past twenty years, we have proven our ability to do so. You might conclude that we have become experts in adaptation and could rise to the level of mastery over the next twenty.

The remainder of Part Three explores a simple needs framework. It includes self-sufficiency, relatedness, purpose, and meaning, and how to satisfy them.

---

110. Source: *The Evolution of a Misquotation,* Darwin Correspondence Project, University of Cambridge https://www.darwinproject.ac.uk/people/about-darwin/six-things-darwin-never-said/evolution-misquotation The fact that he didn't say it doesn't make it less profound.

Chapter 25

Optimizing Your Physical Well-Being and Autonomy

PHYSICAL WELL-BEING and autonomy are table stakes for functioning as a vital and contributing senior. Their pursuit is uniquely personal, and for the most part, must be independently managed. If you haven't made this a priority before now, the moment has arrived.

We have explored numerous dimensions of self-reliance in previous chapters. In simple terms, self-reliance is trusting one's own powers and resources first and foremost. Self-reliance in terms of the aging process is your ability to maintain well-being (physical, psychological, and social), make thoughtful and appropriate decisions in your best interest, and have significant control over the management of your life and living circumstances.

The primary biological and physiological requirements are food, water, clothing, shelter, sanitation, heat, access to medical care, love, and affection, as referenced earlier. Survival requires consistent access to or possession of these requirements. In the absence of physical well-being, the other challenges and consequences of the aging process can become overwhelming.

Autonomy is being mentally and physically capable of navigating your daily life: communicating, making, and keeping commitments, having a view of the world beyond your four walls, a desire to give to and share with others, and an ability and willingness to receive. Although this may sound a bit challenging, be reminded that autonomy is the principal focus for many seniors for the rest of their lives.

We each know seniors who have become hostages to family, friends, state and government workers, caregivers (under many labels), the medical establishment, lenders, and scammers. Autonomy is an antidote, as is belonging to a senior wellness network. This latter solution is the subject of Chapter 29, "The Wellness Forum."

Autonomy requires financial sufficiency during your lifespan. Your independence can be preserved by controlling the resources to pay for your essential requirements. I appreciate that this may not always be possible. But getting as close to it as you can is your best bet for maintaining freedom.

Managing your health is an equally important element of autonomy. Your *healthspan* is the portion of your lifespan when you are generally in good health, free from diseases and chronic conditions among the leading causes of death.[111]

According to the Centers for Disease Control and Prevention (CDC), about *half of all U.S. adults* of all ages (about 125 million people) have one or more chronic health conditions. Over 50 million have two or more such conditions. More than 84% of people aged 65+ are coping with at least one chronic illness, and often more as they age.[112] Seven of the top ten causes of death are chronic diseases: Heart disease is number one, and cancers, number two. Together they account for nearly 46 percent of all U.S. deaths.[113]

111. Source: https://www.ncbi.nlm.nih.gov/pmc/articles/PMC6136295/
112. Source: https://www.ncoa.org/article/get-the-facts-on-senior-debt
113. Source: https://wonder.cdc.gov/controller/saved/D76/D91F186

There has been an alarming increase in the number of people suffering from immune deficiency and autoimmune diseases during our lifetimes. Immune deficiency diseases decrease the body's ability to fight invaders, causing vulnerability to infections. In cases of immune system overactivity, the body attacks and damages its tissues (autoimmune diseases). Some of these include Type 1 diabetes mellitus, rheumatoid arthritis, psoriasis, lupus, multiple sclerosis, myasthenia gravis, celiac disease, inflammatory bowel diseases, and vasculitis. Medical professionals consider these conditions to be among the consequences of abnormal immune responses.[114]

The World Health Organization (WHO) has developed an indicator for healthy life expectancy (HALE).[115] To approximate HALE is to determine the average age of the first occurrence of each of the most common serious diseases, determine their incidences, and then take the average of those two numbers (see the table below). These estimates suggest that, on average, we live up to 20 percent of our lives in an unhealthy state, and unsurprisingly most of this poor health occurs in our senior years.

Disease	Deaths per year	Age of 1st occurrence
Heart Disease	610,000	65
Lung cancer	158,060	60
Chronic obstructive pulmonary disease (COPD)	147,101	45
Stroke	140,000	65
Lower respiratory infections	131,800	75
Alzheimer's disease	93,541	65
Type 2 diabetes	69,071	54
Colorectal cancers	50,260	70
Breast cancer	40,000	62
Prostate cancer	25,000	66

114. Source: www.webmd.com
115. Source: https://publichealth.wustl.edu/heatlhspan-is-more-important-than-lifespan-so-why-dont-more-people-know-about-it/ and http://apps.who.int/gho/data/view.main.HALEXREGv?lang=en

A study published in *The British Medical Journal* looked at years lived without diabetes, cardiovascular disease, or cancer.[116] Researchers examined self-reported data collected from nearly 175,000 healthcare professionals aged 30 to 75. They found that people over 50 who had never smoked, maintained a healthy weight, ate a nutritious diet, regularly exercised, and drank only a moderate amount of alcohol lived about 84 healthy years—a full decade longer than those who did not.

Physical factors that contribute to an extended healthspan include strength, balance, flexibility, and endurance. These elements support your mobility during your life and have an even higher value as you age. Maintaining your mobility is critical for all body functions and is fundamental to avoiding chronic illness. Following is a brief overview of five activities that can keep you moving.

Walking

Walking after meals has been shown to stabilize blood sugar levels. It is also an excellent way to boost metabolism and connect with friends and family. Diabetes and metabolic syndrome are significant contributors to cardiovascular disease and most neurologic disorders, such as dementia.[117] Proper blood sugar and insulin regulation should be a primary concern of anyone desiring to live a long healthy life. Frequent walking is essential.

---

116. Source: https://www.wellandgood.com/increase-healthspan/

117. Metabolic syndrome is not a disease in itself, it is a group of risk factors, including high blood pressure, high blood sugar, unhealthy cholesterol levels, and abdominal fat. According to the American Heart Association, 47 million Americans have it, one out of every six people. The syndrome runs in families and is more common among African Americans, Hispanics, Asians, and Native Americans. The risks of developing metabolic syndrome increase as you age. https://www.webmd.com/heart/metabolic-syndrome/metabolic-syndrome-what-is-it#1

Balance and Floor Mobility

Getting on and off the floor without using your hands is an indicator of your overall strength.[118] The inability to do so correlates closely with early disability and death. We all know of the commercial with the plea, "Help me. I've fallen, and I can't get up!" It is an uncomfortable and scary position. Difficulty balancing translates into lower movement confidence and a downward spiral in mobility: the ability to move or be moved freely and easily. We lose a lot of living options when we become sedentary.

Yoga

Yoga is one of the best forms of exercise for maintaining flexibility and balance and has many other benefits. Some of those are strengthening bones, reducing stress, getting better sleep, and reducing aches and pains. It can also be an antidote to depression. Yoga can be done without any equipment wherever you are. It is also a way to engage with others having a common interest in well-being.

Weight training

Weight training is a critical component in physical resiliency. This exercise category fights off frailty and increases your body's margin for error when illness or injury occurs. Lifting appropriately heavy weights is helpful for almost everyone regardless of age. It has positive benefits on muscle strength, bone density, cardiovascular and neurologic performance and adaptability, mental and cognitive function, and hormonal regulation.[119] It sounds a little strange, I know, to consider starting weight training as a senior, but it is not about bodybuilding contests

118. Source: SixtyandMe.com https://sixtyandme.com/after-60-mobility-is-the-key-to-your-healthspan/
119. Source: https://www.thephysicaltherapyadvisor.com/?s=3%20reasons

or the Olympics. You can begin by doing bicep curls with soup cans. As with all forms of exercise, consult your doctor before you start weight training.

High-intensity interval training (HIIT)

Don't be intimidated by the term high-intensity or the acronym HIIT. Interval training does not require special training or equipment; it can be part of your walking routine. In a study referenced by the Mayo Clinic, walkers who added higher-intensity intervals to their walking program improved their aerobic fitness, leg strength, and blood pressure.[120] They did it by merely alternating three minutes of fast walking and three minutes of slow walking over 30 minutes or more. According to researchers at the Norwegian University of Science and Technology, a twice-a-week routine of high-intensity interval training shows a marked effect on fitness and overall well-being in people over 70.

The more you can integrate these activities into your life, the more likely you will extend your healthspan. Please be sure to consult your doctor before beginning any exercise routine.

As a senior, you know that even starting the physical activities essential to independent living is sometimes challenging. However, others can be a part of the process. You will be surprised how much improvement you can make and how many social connections can come about in just a few months.

My own story: Writing greatly restricts your mobility as you sit for hours a day. As I started this book, I decided to engage more proactively in some of the above-described activities. For over a year, I have averaged four hours a week of fitness training, including weight training (not

---

120. Source: https://www.mayoclinic.org/why-interval-training-may-be-the-best-workout-at-any-age/art-20342125#:~:text=The%20concept%20of%20%22HIIT%22%20is,low%20level%20effort%20of%20exercise

bodybuilding), balance, agility, and mobility exercises. I started slowly and gradually improved in all areas. I also worked up to walking and hiking two to three miles a day.

Early in the process, I saw the benefits of easier breathing, fewer aches and pains, better sleep, greater flexibility, and the disappearance of a few extra pounds. As the months progressed, I added more strength to my core and saw my posture significantly improve. I found myself wanting to pay more attention to my nutrition and get outside for more sunshine-sourced vitamin D. The most significant benefits were a reduction in anxiety and an increase in my energy level.

Anticipating the practical challenges of growing older, I have included exercises that support: standing on one foot long enough to pull on each pant leg without sitting, lifting each leg while seated to put on my socks (and not devolve into a circus act), confidently getting up and down the stairs, getting up off the floor without holding onto anything, and handling grocery bags and packages with ease. These fundamental capabilities provide a foundation for extending your healthspan. You needn't sign on for a marathon or flip a large tractor tire the length of a football field.

Chapter 26

An Even Keel—
Psychological Well-Being

PSYCHOLOGICAL WELL-BEING includes the satisfaction of relatedness, inclusion, self-esteem, and other social needs. It also encompasses the pursuit of mental stability, personal growth, purpose, and meaning. Simply, psychological well-being is about our lives going well. It is a combination of feeling good and functioning effectively.[121]

Even if things are going well for you, monotony, repetitiveness, and isolation can bring unease. Our well-being can be at risk without human connections where we are recognized, heard, mirrored, feel included, relevant, and respected. In the absence of these interactions, it is possible to lose perspective and overthink issues large and small. Reaching out to and connecting with others also is proof of self-reliance and emotional strength.

As you grow older, there comes the point when you want to turn off the voice in your head: the one that has become *even more* of a constant and often irritating companion. It is easy to go off on tangents that are not in your best interest when only listening to (and sometimes conversing with) yourself. Connecting with others is an effective way to get some outside perspective.

---

121. Source: https://iaap-journals.onlinelibrary.wiley.com/doi/full/10.1111/j.1758-0854.2009.01008.x

The spectrum of psychological well-being for seniors should include relatedness, self-esteem, meaning, and purpose. I have distilled and integrated Abraham Maslow's theories (Hierarchy of Needs) and the Psychological Well-Being Model developed by Professor Carol D. Ryff for our purposes. Following are summaries of each. Consider these as touchstones and loose guidelines for pointing you in the direction of your life going well. These summaries are not to be relied upon as professional psychological assessments nor personal counseling.

Maslow's Hierarchy of Needs

Maslow's Hierarchy of Needs is the best known. He postulates that people have a hierarchy of needs to be satisfied in sequence from bottom to top. These begin with physiological subsistence and safety needs (physical well-being), progress to social relatedness and self-esteem (psychological well-being), then advance to the pursuit of self-actualization (a sense of purpose and meaning). Maslow believed that unfulfilled needs lower on the pyramid would inhibit moving to the next level. Later commentary, including Clayton Alderfer's Existence, Relatedness, Growth (ERG) Theory, made the case that a sequential approach was unnecessary.

Maslow's hierarchy includes *deficiency needs* (physiological, safety, social, and self-esteem) and *growth needs* (meaning, purpose, and self-actualization). The deficiency needs are typically an individual's responsibility but may require some degree of relatedness to others. If the deficiency needs are not satisfied, pursuing the growth needs (self-fulfillment) could be stifled.

The Psychological Well-Being Model

I found Professor Carol D. Ryff's Psychological Well-Being model highly relevant and straightforward. She identified six foundation elements for well-being and created a method for assessing them. Following is a description of the relative values established for each.[122]

Autonomy

A person exhibiting autonomy embraces decision-making based upon their interests. Autonomy represents a sense of, "I have confidence in my decisions and opinions, even if they are contrary to the consensus." Ryff does not explicitly reference fundamental physiological requirements. However, the elements of physical well-being and a foundation of financial self-sufficiency are critical to autonomy.

A high scorer in autonomy on a Ryff assessment exhibits self-determination, independence, and the ability to resist social pressures to think and act in specific ways. They can self-regulate behavior and have developed personal standards and methods of confidently evaluating and managing through various conditions. The individual feels no need to defend, explain, or rationalize their actions for others' benefit. They are open-minded. Anything that someone else might say is open for consideration.

Another dimension of autonomy includes being at peace with yourself and others, including those who might disagree or even threaten you. You do not fear losing the admiration of others. Therefore, you do not have to be 'right.' You may interpret this dimension as encompassing self-reliance.

A lower scorer on the autonomy dimension of the Ryff scale believes that difficulties and problems result from events and things outside of

---

122. For ease of introduction, a high scorer's attributes are juxtaposed with those of lower scorers. I have added references to concepts previously addressed in this book that I believe relate to Ryff's model. I have also reordered the typical presentation of the dimensions cited by Ryff and supplemented the descriptions with my views of related values and concepts.

them. "It is beyond my control," or, "It is your fault, not mine." We are out-of-integrity with ourselves when we explain our difficulties and problems as a function of external circumstances beyond our control.[123]

The fact that we may be the source of these difficulties and problems is invisible to us. A low scorer is concerned about others' expectations and evaluations and may rely more heavily on outside judgments in making decisions. They are likely to conform to social pressures to think and act in specific ways.

Environmental Mastery

Environmental mastery has two dimensions: The Bigger Picture world-view and the more localized environment in which individuals conduct their daily lives.

A high scorer in environmental mastery has a sense of competence and confidence in managing their environment. They work through a complex array of external inputs and activities, make effective use of opportunities within reach, and choose or create contexts that enable personal satisfaction of needs and desires.

A lower scorer has difficulty managing everyday affairs, feels unable to change or improve their surrounding context, is unaware of potential opportunities, and has a somewhat vague sense of control over the external world.

---

123. Source: *Integrity: A Positive Model that Incorporates the Normative Phenomena of Morality, Ethics and Legality,* https://papers.ssrn.com/sol3/papers.cfm?abstract_id=920625

Self-Acceptance

A self-accepting individual has a positive self-attitude, is not overly self-critical nor confused about their identity. Typically, they do not aspire to be different than they are.

A high scorer acknowledges and accepts all their aspects, including the good and bad qualities. They are satisfied with their personal history and are more likely to say, "I like most aspects of my personality."

A lower scorer has a lesser sense of independence and freedom and often feels dissatisfied. They may be self-critical, disappointed with what occurred throughout their lives, more risk-averse and fearful of failure, and want to be someone other than themselves.

Positive Relations with Others

This dimension encompasses the possession of quality connections and relationships with others, i.e., "People would describe me as a giving person, willing to share my time with others." These qualities may manifest in positive expressions of obligation, responsibility, companionship, intimacy, and love.

A high scorer on the Ryff scale will possess warm, satisfying, trusting relationships with others, show concern for their welfare, is capable of empathy, affection, and intimacy, and understands the give and take of relationships.

A low scorer will exhibit few close, trusting relationships with others. Generally, they find it difficult to be warm, open, and concerned about them. They may present as isolated and frustrated in interpersonal relationships. They may seem rigid, i.e., unwilling to make compromises to sustain ties with others.

Personal Growth

Personal growth is a sense of continued development as a person, i.e., "I think it is important to have new experiences that challenge how I think about myself and the world." You could think of it, in part, as pursuing the realization of potential.

Carl Rogers, one of the fathers of humanistic psychology, observed that people who make real progress toward what can be considered a 'life going well' would typically *not* regard themselves as happy or contented. He states, "The good life is a process, not a state of being." It suggests a sense of daily renewal required for sustaining a commitment, as reviewed in Chapter 21.

A high scorer in personal growth pursues such a process and continued individual development. They see growth and expansion in themselves and recognize the improvement. They are open to new experiences, have a sense of realizing their potential, and adapt in ways that reflect self-knowledge and effectiveness.

In this dimension, a low scorer has a sense of personal stagnation, does not feel a sense of improvement or expansion over time, may be bored and uninterested in life, and finds it challenging to develop or adopt new attitudes or behaviors.

Purpose in Life

A purpose in life is having a belief that one's life is progressive and meaningful. These individuals discover a sense of purpose in striving for change, a better understanding of themselves and the world, and a desire to grow and become better in their chosen domains of life.

A high scorer in this dimension of Ryff's assessment has a sense of directedness, finds meaning in their current and past life, holds beliefs that give life purpose, and has goals and objectives for living. They might say, "Some people aimlessly wander through life, but I am not one of them."

A low scorer lacks a sense of direction and meaning, has few goals, does not see a life purpose or value, and is devoid of an outlook or beliefs that enable the pursuit of a life of meaning.

A later study conducted by Ryff indicated that persons who aspired more for financial success than affiliation with others scored lower on various well-being measures.[124] If you need additional motivation to do the work to eliminate the concern for financial security in your life, this could be it. Economic sufficiency and satisfaction are among the gateways to well-being.

Research conducted by Howard Friedman (best known for his pioneering work on Type A personalities and cardiac problems) and Margaret Kern indicated that higher levels of conscientiousness are associated with living longer and better. Conscientiousness is a composite of responsibility, self-control, achievement, and order. They concluded that conscientious individuals are less likely to die prematurely than others in the same age range.

In *The Time Paradox*, authors Philip Zimbardo and John Boyd articulate that future-oriented people are more likely than all others to engage in positive health behaviors and not engage in health-threatening behaviors. They conclude that negative health-related behavior patterns set the stage for an individual to die sooner. A shift toward being a future-oriented creator of personal well-being offers an opportunity to live longer and better.

124. Sources: Ryff, Carol D. and Keyes, Lee M., "The Structure of Psychological Well-Being Revisited," American Psychological Association, *Journal of Personality and Social Psychology*, 1995, Vol.69, No. 4, 719-727, and Ryff, Carol D. and Singer, Burton, "Psychological Well-Being: Meaning, Measurement, and Implications for Psychotherapy Research," *Psychotherapy and Psychosomatics*, 1996:65:14-23.

Psychological well-being, the state of our lives going well, can be explored through individual conscientiousness and the manifestation of the positive behaviors outlined above. In your feelings of positivity, comfort, certainty, mindfulness, and resilience, you can find a sense of personal progress. Do you feel you are progressing upward in the Maslow hierarchy and have a closer alignment with a high scorer's profiles on each of Ryff's dimensions? If so, you likely are on your way to a heightened sense of psychological well-being.

My path as a senior involves more reflection. This activity helps me process feelings I still carry from previous events and relationships. Unhooking from those is sometimes challenging and consumes more of today's energy than I would like. I know that perspectives offered by history can be valuable. But, I also recognize that the environment today is much different than when those experiences took place.

Challenge the events from your personal history that still constrain you. Give full attention to your world of today. Accepting, "It was what it was," coupled with recognition of what cannot be changed, keeps your focus on your immediate and future well-being.

Chapter 27

The Benefits of Seeking Purpose and Meaning

BEING OUTER-DIRECTED is, for the most part, our point of view during the first half or two-thirds of our lives.

This attention goes first to our parents, extended family, age group peers, teachers, and professors.

Second, to career, living circumstances, potential life partners, social companions, and possibly children. Making a living typically dominates this phase of life. We strive to pay for our essentials and acquire other material possessions that may be desirable or within our grasp.

Third, we complete the raising of our families, our time in the workforce, and perhaps even slow our pursuit of status and material things. Suddenly, we may find that the noise level and the clutching of the outside world have considerably lessened. Then, just ahead, the remainder of our lives comes into view.

In our middle years, in addition to outer-directed, we may become more *other-directed*. Colin Wilson described an other-directed individual as one "...conditioned by society to lack self-confidence in their ability to achieve anything of real worth, and thus they conform to society to escape their feelings of unimportance and uselessness." [125] He calls this the fallacy of insignificance.

Conformity is a social panacea for coping with such perceived insignificance and unrealized potential. We expend much of our time and potential being other- and outer-directed, and 'conforming.'

As the mileposts of our lives rushed by, we found it progressively more challenging to find quiet moments for personal reflection—for putting our existence into the context of the predictable passages of life. The numbing march for financial sufficiency, other than sleep, consumed the bulk of our adult lifetimes. In most surveys of seniors asking them about regrets, a dominant response is, "I wish I hadn't worked so much or so hard."

We may occasionally find ourselves scanning the world immediately around us for a shred of objective recognition that we are worthy of someone's attention. If you place too much value on the scant feedback, if any, you receive, the feeling of insignificance that motivated your search will be reinforced rather than relieved.

As humans, we typically confront the issue of our relative importance at some point. We now find ourselves individually as 1 of 8,000,000,000 living souls on the planet. It is no wonder we seek to create stories of why we are significant.

Astronomer Carl Sagan, describing the human inhabitants of our pale blue dot,[126] said, "...our posturings, our imagined self-importance, and the delusion that we [individually] have some privileged position in the Universe," are rendered nonsensical by comparison.[127]

---

125. Colin Wilson was was an English writer, philosopher, novelist, and author of *The Stature of Man.*

126. The Pale Blue Dot is a photograph of planet Earth taken on February 14, 1990, by the Voyager 1 space probe from a record distance of about 6 billion kilometers.

127. Source: Carl Sagan, *Pale Blue Dot: A Vision of the Human Future in Space,* and https://www.amazon.com/Pale-Blue-Dot-Vision-Future/dp/0345376595

I decided to test the issue of our relative earthly physical significance. "What is the cubic volume of the Earth's entire population?" I asked. As luck would have it, there were a few relevant search returns. I found an entertaining analysis by Phil Plait, self-described astronomer, author, and science communicator. Here is his answer:

> Humans are almost exactly the same density as water... Water has a density of 1 gram per cubic centimeter ("cc". For comparison, 1 cc is very roughly half the volume of the tip of your pinky to the first knuckle... the average volume of a human is 62,000 cubic centimeters. To get the total volume of all Earthly humans, just multiply that by 7.6 billion [now 7.8]. This equals 470 [now 515] trillion cubic centimeters.[128]

The volume of all earthly humanity would fit in a cube roughly half a mile (770 meters) on each side. Fortunately, Phil created a black cube graphic juxtaposed against San Francisco's Golden Gate Bridge, which makes the point.[129] Yes, based upon Phil's assumptions, all humans could fit in such a cube.

Credit: Crew and Officers of NOAA Ship MILLER FREEMAN / Phil Plait

---

128. Source: https://www.syfy.com/syfywire/the-human-cube-the-volume-of-humanity#:~:text=Thepercent20averagepercent20humanpercent20haspercent20a,apercent20weirdpercent20amountpercent20topercent20grasp

129. Phil Plait's friend, Randall Munroe suggested you could submerge the cube in the ocean and see how much the level of the water goes up. He calculated that the submersion yields an increase of one micron in sea level, a millionth of a meter, or 1/100th the width of a human hair. Randall also found in four hours, the impact of global warming adds more to the sea level rise than does dumping all humans into the ocean.

Many scientific descriptions and illustrations show the insignificance of individual humans compared with the scale of the universe. Whether on Earth or in the cosmos, we cannot make a credible argument that we are significant in the physical dimension.

Once the outer- and other-directed attention in our lives has diminished to some degree, we may discover something inside us that is worth exploring. You might call it your inner capital. These resources may have been overlooked or viewed as of lesser value for a lifetime.[130]

Viewing our significance through our subjectivity lens is lending one of our best human characteristics to this effort. The only judge of the value of these assets need be you. Your inner capital can be insignificant or priceless, determined solely through your assessment and assignment of relative value.

The founder of analytical psychology, Carl Jung, shifted the aging concept from gradual but inevitable decline (and withdrawal from the mainstream) to active engagement and contributing to society. He said, "The afternoon of human life must also have a significance of its own and cannot merely be a pitiful appendage to life's morning." This change in the perspective of aging from deficiency and loss to the use of our latent inner capital to pursue spiritual and psychological growth can be life-changing.

Jung referred to this process of turning inward as *individuation*. Think of it as an exploration of your inner capital. Recognizing individuation as a process and not an event offers the opportunity for confirmation of our lives' value and significance throughout our senior years. Jung said, "A greater depth of self-understanding will help [us]... better tolerate the ambiguity and paradoxes of aging and affirm the value of life in the

---

130. The first time I took notice of the term inner capital was when my friend and former colleague, Katie Pushor, used it as the name for her leadership consulting business. www.innercapitalaz.com

face of good and evil, pain and joy, and the other oppositions that mark our existence." When better to indulge our subjectivity than in the process of discovering personal significance?

The creator of the theory of gerotranscendence was Lars Tornstam, a professor of social gerontology at Uppsala University in Sweden. He found that successfully aging individuals undergo a perspectival shift that leads to significant changes. He chronicled self-perception changes from materialistic and rational to more intangible ones.[131] The latter he refers to as "cosmic."

Interviews with individuals between 52 and 97 years of age supported his conclusions. He found that changes during aging occur at three levels:

Self
   • A decreased obsession with one's body.
   • A decreased interest in material things.
   • A decrease in self-centeredness.
   • An increased desire to understand oneself.
   • An increased desire for inner peace and meditation.
   • An increased need for solitude.

Personal and Social Relationships

   • A decreased desire for prestige.
   • A decreased desire for superfluous, superficial social interaction.
   • A decreased interest in conforming to social roles.
   • An increased concern for others.
   • An increased need for solitude or the company of only a few intimates.

---

131. Source: Lars Tornstam, *Gerotranscendence* | *Reason and Meaning*. https://reasonandmeaning.com/2020/09/10/lars-tornstam-on-gerotranscendence/

- An increased selectivity in the choice of social and other activities.
- An increased level of spontaneity that moves beyond social norms.
- An increase in broadmindedness and tolerance.
- An increased sense of life's ambiguity.

Cosmic

- A decreased distinction between past and present.
- A decreased fear of death.
- An increased affinity with, and interest in, past and future generations.
- An increased acceptance of the mysteries of human life.
- An increased joy over small or insignificant things.
- An increased appreciation of nature.
- An increased feeling of communion with the universe and cosmic awareness.

The Tornstam interviews confirm that the balance in aging ultimately tips in the direction of continued growth, purpose, and meaning. Seniors should be willing to surrender their youthful identities to achieve maturity and wisdom.

Pursuing individual purpose can help people face uncertainties and better navigate them. In *Igniting Individual Purpose in Times of Crisis*,[132] the authors wrote:

---

132. Source: Naina Dhingra, Jonathan Emmett, Andrew Samo, and Bill Schaninger, *Igniting Individual Purpose in Times of Crisis*, McKinsey & Company, August 18, 2020, and https://www.mckinsey.com/business-functions/organization/our-insights/igniting-individual-purpose-in-times-of-crisis?cid=other-eml-alt-mcq-mck&hlkid=9f57d7be151842c8b0bed2bab1583635&hctky=1260186&hdpid=63c53581-962d-4126-9425-78effc837881

People who have a strong sense of purpose tend to be more resilient and exhibit better recovery from negative events. Indeed, our research conducted during the [Covid-19] pandemic finds that when comparing people who say they are "living their purpose" at work, with those who say they aren't, the former report levels of well-being that are five times higher than the latter. Moreover, those in the former group are four times more likely to report higher engagement levels.

> Purposeful people also live longer and healthier lives. One longitudinal study found that a single standard deviation [improvement] in purpose decreased the risk of dying over the next decade by 15 percent—*a finding that held regardless of the age at which people identified their purpose.* [Emphasis added.]

> Similarly, the Rush Memory and Aging Project, which began in 1997, found that when comparing patients who say they have a sense of purpose with those who say they don't, the former are 2.5 times more likely to be free of dementia, 22 percent less likely to exhibit risk factors for stroke, and 52 percent less likely to have experienced a stroke.

Viktor Frankl said, "Life is never made unbearable by circumstances, but only by lack of meaning and purpose." Pursuing meaning and purpose in your senior years can deepen your feelings of aliveness. In the process, perhaps you will discover the purpose that may outlive your consciousness.

Chapter 28

Social Self-Reliance— Trusting in Others

SOME RARE INDIVIDUALS create prosperous lives through the near-exclusive pursuit of solitude and isolation. I still prefer a quiet life with lots of reflective time. But I discovered that I must incorporate giving to and receiving from others as an essential part of living. I now see that the value in "I" and "me" can be expanded by the inclusion, belonging, and more significant potential of "we" and "us." With this recognition, I also realized that I could enrich my life through greater service to others.

Self-reliance in the chaotic and complex world we operate in today must include the knowledge, reflection, and resonance of others similarly situated. This inclusion of others is *social self-reliance*, a now necessary extension of individual self-reliance.

Charles Darwin said, "In the long history of humankind (and animal kind, too), those who learned to collaborate and improvise most effectively have prevailed." Collaboration is a way to reduce the personal impact of the chaos and ambiguity outside us. It is essential for realizing your potential in a perpetually dynamic external environment.

Social self-reliance recognizes that as much as you must look to yourself for your fundamental living requirements, it will not produce everything you need. A full measure of self-reliance includes a connection with others to help supply the missing pieces. In consideration of their help, you help them reduce their discomfort and uncertainty, thereby closing the fulfillment gaps in their lives. Maya Angelou said, "As you grow older, you will discover that you have two hands, one for helping yourself, the other for helping others."

Difficult or even dire circumstances can and do bring people together in ways that would otherwise be impossible. As a part of significant external shifts, our relationships with family members can evolve to produce a different kind of care and concern, often more authentic. We may find ourselves unexpectedly connecting and bonding with our friends, neighbors, and co-workers to address similar requirements. We may find value in discovering and getting to know people new to our lives for the same reasons.

Michael A. Hogg, a professor and chair of social psychology at Claremont Graduate University, put it this way. "People need to have a firm sense of identity and their place in the world, and for many, the pace and magnitude of [today's] change can be alienating. Our sense of self is a fundamental organizing principle for our own perceptions, feelings, attitudes, and actions... *[Another] powerful source of identity resides in social groups. They can be highly effective at reducing a person's self-uncertainty...*"[133] [Emphasis added.]

Whether you create these kinds of social connections with one person, a few, or a group, think of it as constructing a wellness network for yourself. Wellness is the quality or state of being healthy in body and mind. A *wellness network* is a vehicle for learning, growing, and connecting to strive for such good health. It represents harnessing the power of a cooperative group, even just a few people, to deepen and extend your self-reliance.

---

133. Source: Michael A. Hogg, "The Search for Social Identity Leads to 'Us' Versus 'Them,'" *Scientific American*, September 2019, https://www.scientificamerican.com/article/the-search-for-social-identity-leads-to-us-versus-them/

A wellness network could consist of some existing friends, repurposed current groups, or creating a more formal Wellness Forum (described below). Such a group could begin simply as a meet-up with a trusted friend, or a few, to discuss current events. These connections will result in some relatedness moments and the expansion of perspectives.

Such a collective could be a natural extension of an existing group or sub-group of people with a common interest. For example, it might include friends and acquaintances from your church, a book club, a bridge group, a bowling team, current or former coworkers, fellow residents of a neighborhood, apartment building, residential living facility, military unit, membership associations, or fellow inmates in prison.

No one should have to deal alone with the attacks from external threats, including a new form of a pandemic or more waves of social unrest and political divisiveness. David Brooks wrote, "When Americans were confronted [in the context of Covid-19] with the extremely hard task of locking down for months without any of the collective resources that would have made it easier—habits of deference to group needs; a dense network of community bonds to help hold each other accountable; a history of trust that if you do the right thing, others will too; preexisting patterns of cooperation; a sense of shame if you deviate from the group—they couldn't do it..."[134]

What we learn and do today will set the stage for meaningful social and community support when, not if, the next life-changing blow comes along.

---

134. Source: https://www.theatlantic.com/ideas/archive/2020/10/collapsing-levels-trust-are-devastating-america/616581/.

Chapter 29

The Wellness Forum

FULFILLMENT GAPS EXIST across your spectrum of personal needs. You can fill them by reaching outside the limits of your self-sufficiency. This extension is engaging in social self-reliance. The principles and objectives are the same whether you choose to connect with a few people, a small existing group, or more.

I will use the vehicle of a more formalized Wellness Forum to suggest approaches that will also work for the more casual collectives of wellness networks. The objective is to enable a higher level of person-to-person interaction and relatedness. These ideas will allow you to create a wellness network in a form that fits your circumstances and personality. What you choose to call it doesn't matter.

A Wellness Forum is a social collective dedicated to the pursuit of well-being for its members and service to others. The members who agree to be a part of a Wellness Forum support each other in striving for wholeness, a combination of the personal (self-reliance) and the collective (social self-reliance).

This Forum is the embodiment of the statement, "I have to do it myself, but I cannot do it alone." The Wellness Forum offers the opportunity to contribute your knowledge, experiences, and uniqueness to others. It also opens the door to receiving those gifts from others.

What you once did for work, where you lived, what you drove, and where you vacationed are less relevant as a senior—perhaps even irrelevant. You might be a billionaire or a retired dishwasher. The question for both is how to live in a state of wellness consistently. More importantly, as a part of serving others, how will you use what you have and know?

A crucial element in the creation of a Wellness Forum is the selection of the members.[135] Think of the process of formation of this group as selecting an advisory board for your life. In assembling a business board of directors, we look to recruit and onboard people with different backgrounds, work and life experiences, education, and personalities. Individuals with expertise in areas that match current and future business needs will be better candidates, all things being equal.

You could apply the same process in forming a Wellness Forum. You might include someone with a healthcare background: a physician's assistant, nurse or another caregiver, or a medical office staffer. Another member might have experience in bookkeeping, banking, or investments. Others might know something about contracts, housing issues, employment, politics, or nutrition. Each of the potential members will know people who could bring other attributes needed for a well-rounded, hyperlocal community of well-being.

Each member will come into the Wellness Forum with education, expertise, work, and life experiences that reflect their uniqueness. They will have varied interests, avocations, and hobbies. The group will represent a mosaic of individual stories to share with others. The charter for each Wellness Forum should match the needs of and accommodate the membership's common and agreed-upon interests.

A Wellness Forum can be a clearinghouse for information and knowledge of value to its members, their friends and families, and others. It can

---

135. I hereafter refer to the individuals in a Wellness Forum as "members."

improve the members' ability to deal with aging challenges by exploring the issues together. The priorities and topics will vary based on the group's composition, interests, and current events in the community, nation, and world.

To this end, each person could be responsible for sharing daily or weekly news clips and summaries about specific areas of their interest. Examples could include local and national politics, environmental issues, weather, travel, seminars and events, health tips, cooking, gardening (food and landscape), exercising, and other topics. You could agree upon a weekly subject for conversation (a roundtable discussion) with relevance for some or all the group members.

The members might choose to have a periodic conversation about a book or an article. They might determine to watch a YouTube video, TED Talk, or a new or old movie and discuss it. You could invite an outside speaker. The potential for thriving among individuals committed to lifelong learning is unlimited.

This interchange is vital for broadening the curiosity and breadth of knowledge of the group. Maintaining mental acuity and vitality is tied to staying curious and sharing with the other group members. A Wellness Forum can be a center for such sharing, challenge, and conversation, beyond ailments and personal laments. These should be parked at the door unless otherwise agreed.

The evidence suggests that younger generations will face more disorder, anxiety, and financial sufficiency challenges than ours. They will need the help of trusted peers even more than we do. Please discuss the concept of social self-reliance with the younger people in your life and suggest they form wellness networks.

Chapter 30

You Can Count on Me

DETERMINING THE VALUES of a Wellness Forum is crucial to its governance and success. Trust, integrity, and kindness must be among them. These values represent guiding principles for interactions among the individuals in the group and for the collective.

A commitment to these values can make the Wellness Forum a safe harbor from the falseness and fakery found almost everywhere else. Writer David Brooks wrote, "... social trust is built within organizations in which people are bound together to do joint work, in which they struggle together long enough for trust to gradually develop, in which they develop shared understandings of what is expected of each other, in which they are enmeshed in rules and standards of behavior that keep them trustworthy when their commitments might otherwise falter..."[136]

Pew Research Center surveyed over 10,000 Americans over three years about their levels of trust and confidence. Pew summarized, "Two-thirds of adults think other Americans have little or no confidence in the federal government. Majorities believe the public's confidence in the U.S. government and each other is shrinking, and most believe a

---

136. Source: https://www.theatlantic.com/ideas/archive/2020/10/collapsing-levels-trust-are-devastating-america/616581/

shortage of trust in government and citizens makes it harder to solve some of the nation's key problems."[137]

Other conclusions from the Pew studies:

- Fading trust is a sign of cultural sickness and national decline. Some tie it to increased loneliness and excessive individualism.
- About half of Americans link the decline in interpersonal trust to a belief that people are not as reliable as they used to be. They also call out others' traits such as laziness, greed, and dishonesty.
- A share of the public believes toxic national politics and polarization have taken their toll on Americans' way of thinking.
- Adults ages 18 to 29 stand out for their comparatively low levels of trust. Around three-quarters of U.S. adults under 30 believe people "just look out for themselves" most of the time. Seventy-one percent said most people "would try to take advantage of you if they got a chance," and six-in-ten say most people "can't be trusted."[138]

This latter point is interesting because more than 50 percent of today's 18 to 29-year-old adult population live with their parents (the highest rate since the Great Depression). While under that roof, two-thirds of them indicate they do not trust their parents and believe they would try to take advantage of them if they could. "Welcome home. Happy you are here."

Americans offer one positive assessment in this otherwise challenging environment: they believe *they* are trustworthy. Some 98 percent of high trusters, 93 percent of medium trusters, and 79 percent of low trusters agree with the statement, "Most people trust [me]."

---

137. Source: file:///C:/Users/Wm%20K/Downloads/PEW-RESEARCH-CENTER_ TRUST-DISTRUST-IN-AMERICA-REPORT_2019-07-22-1%20(1).pdf
138. Source: https://www.pewresearch.org/fact-tank/2019/08/06/young-americans-are-less-trusting-of-other-people-and-key-institutions-than-their-elders/

Lisa B. Kwan, a senior researcher at Harvard University, wrote an article about security in cross-group business collaboration.[139] I see her theory as applicable to effective collaboration within a wellness network and Wellness Forum.

She concluded that a sense of security exists along three dimensions. Firstly, the group must have an identity. Its *raison d'être* must be sufficiently clear so the members can feel secure that they are in the right place to achieve their objectives. Secondly, the group must have legitimacy based upon the trust granted by each member, as well as external perceptions of the group as a value creator. Thirdly, the group's security is contingent upon its ability to control and manage its processes and outcomes. A commitment to security enables the group to effect meaningful change and do so in an orderly way.

The members' integrity is required for trust, security, and kindness to develop within the collective. In *Integrity: A Positive Model that Incorporates the Normative Phenomena of Morality, Ethics and Legality*,[140] the authors Werner Erhard, Michael C. Jensen, and Steve Zaffron wrote:

> For an individual we distinguish integrity as a matter of that person's word being whole and complete. For a group or organizational entity, we define integrity as that group's or organization's word being whole and complete. A group's or organization's word consists of what is said between the people in that group or organization...

> By "keeping your word" we mean doing what you said you would do and by the time you said you would do it...

---

139. Source: https://hbr.org/2019/03/the-collaboration-blind-spot?autocomplete=true
140. Source: https://papers.ssrn.com/sol3/papers.cfm?abstract_id=920625

Honoring your word is also the route to creating whole and complete social and working relationships. In addition, it provides an actionable pathway to earning the trust of others... to being whole and complete with oneself, or in other words to being an integrated person.

Forming and maintaining a Wellness Forum is first about the values of trust, integrity, and kindness. If you cannot honor your word as your minimum contribution and commitment to the Wellness Forum, you should simply go your own way. Compromising these core values will undercut the group's value to all members.

The previous chapters' descriptions relating to physical well-being and autonomy, psychological well-being, and relatedness should be considered an introduction. My objective was to provide enough information to consider learning more about these kinds of needs in your life.

Chapter 31

"What is the Meaning of Life?"

WELLNESS NETWORKS AND Wellness Forums can serve individual well-being, purpose, and meaning. Viktor Frankl and others have pointed out that meaning does not exist in a void—it requires active engagement with others. These social groups can represent a context for your exploration of meaning and purpose in living, as well as a vehicle for making contributions to the greater societal good.

Philosophical theories—the logic and explanations offered to explain our place in the human condition—can be dense and almost incomprehensible. But at some point, questions come up that once did not seem relevant or essential. Some of these could be *existential questions.*

Existential questions help us examine our living experiences and assess our relative value, purpose, and meaning. A core existential question is, "What is the meaning of my existence?" This inquiry and others like it often come up when the process of living may have created disorder, confusion, and anxiety. They could come up because of aging.

Some of the common existential questions include:

- Who am I?
- Why do I exist?
- What is my real nature?

- What is my greater purpose?
- What is the meaning of life?
- Did my life matter?
- What is death?
- Is this all there is?

We put aside these questions in favor of almost anything and every-thing else as we rushed through our lives. Considering these inquiries is not a priority when our lives' environmental, social, cultural, political, and financial challenges have us tied up in knots. Part of the reason for addressing those issues in Parts One and Two was to free you to address these more philosophical questions.

I suspect that a significant number of the 95,000,000+ Americans ages 55 and over have or will engage in these kinds of inquiries. It would be nice to simply ask and answer, "Did my life have meaning? Absolutely. Period. Check. Let's move on." But these questions, when answered, almost always raise others that undercut any short and facile answers. An obvious next question is, "How can I know? Where is the proof?"

Asking these questions and attempting to answer them can be daunting. One approach is to use the previously suggested sentence stem and completion exercises. Following are some questions to work with as a first step toward a more in-depth existential inquiry if you choose it.

- My existence so far has mainly...
- If others were asked about you, "Who is s/he?" the top comments...
- At my core, I am naturally...
- If the life I have lived so far is all that there is...
- As it relates to others, I see meaning in their lives...
- Before I die, I want to deal with feelings of regret about...

Here is yet another reminder of the approach: Complete six different endings for each of the stems. Do not censor yourself or edit the results. You are tapping into what you already know. If you draw a blank, invent an ending. Just get something down on paper. Complete each one as quickly as possible, then put them away for two days.

Keep the questions in the back of your mind and allow other thoughts to arise. (Consider using the tool of differentiation discussed earlier.) When you view your answers again, add as many additional endings as you can.

This process could be the start of your inquiry into the existential questions that matter most to you. It may never be complete, but you will have actively engaged in the process of discovering the *essential you* that you may have never fully seen. If you are comfortable sharing this inquiry with others, you could discuss it with a few friends or in the Wellness Forum as a group exercise (with or without sharing your answers). There may be value in hearing how others are working through the answers to the questions, and you may find some ideas for yourself.

Individual engagement in these inquires ties directly to self-reliance. The value of this process will be your self-assessment and consideration of your answers. If you cannot find answers in the specific context of your life and experiences, perhaps you will find meaning in contemplating the questions.

Ultimately, I wish for you to be able to move on to another question, "What more is needed in this moment?" Go ahead and ask it now, and immediately answer. You will feel a stillness and realize that you have nothing to say. You will feel an appreciation for the completeness of the current moment. Your inability to identify anything lacking represents the discovery of a great truth: "Nothing more is needed in this moment. It is perfect as it is."

For the most part, my life has been a series of moments stitched together, sometimes haphazardly. In moments of happiness, I feel I possess everything I need. I am grateful for the ability to notice and appreciate them, as they have eluded me for most of my life.

"Nothing more is needed in this moment." The existential questions, consideration of your relative value and worthiness as a human, and the other external pulls on you—all are stilled. When you notice that you feel happy, you possess fulfillment that the answers to the biggest of existential questions cannot match. An answer to the question, "Who am I, really?" could be, "At this moment, I am happy."

Chapter 32

How to Leave a Legacy

HUMANS HAVE A desire to live. We also want to believe our time on Earth made a difference. Although we are aware that we represent a tiny and irrelevant presence in the physical universe, we want to feel valued, even if only for ourselves and a very few others.

Consider these thoughts shared by Charles Murray in a lecture entitled, "The Happiness of the People:"

> To become a source of deep satisfaction, a human activity has to meet some stringent requirements. It has to have been important (we don't get deep satisfaction from trivial things). You have to have put a lot of effort into it (hence the cliché "nothing worth having comes easily"). And you have to have been responsible for the consequences.

> There aren't many activities in life that can satisfy those three requirements. Having been a good parent. That qualifies. A good marriage. That qualifies. Having been a good neighbor and good friend to those whose lives intersected with yours. That qualifies. And having been really good at something—good at something that drew the most from your abilities. That qualifies.

To best learn, we typically must experience things firsthand, whether children or adults. "Don't touch the stove. It's hot!" Rather than trusting the advice of those who came before us, we often prefer to repeat their mistakes. If you could hear the views of a group of people ages 95 and older about what they would do if they could live their lives again, perhaps listening would be a good idea. It might be preferable to waiting until it is too late for you to attempt a do-over.[141]

Dr. Anthony Campolo, a college professor, asked fifty people, each of whom were at least 95 years old, "If you could live your life over, what would you do differently?" The top findings were:

Take More Risk

They would have taken more risk when they had the opportunities to do so. If they could have re-set their aging clock to 60 or 75, they would be prepared to move through fear and take more chances. They would welcome opportunities to push outside their comfort zones, even just a bit more.

How can you incorporate the advice of "take more risk?" What if you decided that just for the next month when your inner voice says, "No, I am not doing this because I am afraid," you answer, "I will try it although it feels uncomfortable." If a month is too long, try for a week or even a day.

Wouldn't it be great to be interviewed on your 95th birthday and be able to say, "I did everything I wanted to do by getting outside of my comfort zone, and I started doing it at age 75!" The best could be yet to come.

---

141. This section is an adaptation of a passage in my book, *Life Expectancy, It's Never Too Late to Change your Game.*

More Time for Reflection

The nonagenarians would have reflected more on what was going on in their lives as the days passed. While living each day, they would have spent time contemplating the deeper meaning of life, family, work, and much more.

If you are 65 and look ahead to turning 95, you have 30 years of opportunity for both doing and reflecting. Another option would be to watch TV and allow years to tick away. Then what? Regrets, rather than celebrating those 30 years, your contributions made, and wisdom acquired?

Reflection is noticing that you need not wind down or check out because you are 55 or 75 or 82. You have a life ahead that can count for something if you make it so. Consider what it can be and make a plan. It does not have to be deep or complicated. It just must be your creation.

Create a Legacy

They confirmed the value of a legacy—a way of leaving a contribution indicating "I was here, remember!" It might not (and probably won't) be a multimillion-dollar donation, or a valuable piece of art left to a charity. But it could be a letter left for your family or friends or gifting a book that best reflects your beliefs about life.

You can create a legacy statement or letter by completing at least six complete sentences using the following sentence stems. Remember to put your ideas down as quickly as you can. You can work with them more later.

- People will remember me because…
- The three things that I consider my life accomplishments…
- During my lifetime, I am proudest…
- In twenty years, the one thing people may remember…

- This story that best represents my commitment to my family...
- In terms of my character, I have been told over-and-over...
- In my career, the solutions that will live on...
- The one contribution I have made that people do not know...
- Outside of my friends and family, I believe I made the most impact...
- If I could offer money or other material possessions as a legacy, I would leave...

Considering these questions may reveal ideas about a potential legacy and even affect how you live the rest of your life.

Another way to approach this is to put together a small book of your reflections (books with blank pages are readily available). These could contain:

- Highlights of key events of your life on a timeline.
- A description of some of your ancestors and what you know about them.
- Some of the quotes, sayings, Bible verses, music, or recipes that you value.
- Your favorite memories of each of your children, spouse, pets, and friends.
- Cards and letters that meant something special.
- Photos that you treasured.
- Some of the legacy questions and your answers.
- Letters to be delivered.
- Video or audio recordings you made.

You can offer a legacy through your words and actions in serving others: time and attention, empathy and kindness, love and affection, patience and understanding, and simply being ready and willing to lend a helping hand. Because you may be more personally challenged in your senior years, serving others will leave a lasting impression.

Whether you create a legacy letter, a book or this work stimulates a conversation with others about it (perhaps in a family gathering or a Wellness Forum), what will outlast you is the impact you had on others' lives. Albert Pike wrote in *Ex Corde Locutiones,* "What we have done for ourselves alone, dies with us; what we have done for others and the world remains and is immortal." This sort of impact is a legacy, whether the person leaving it is Abraham Lincoln, Mother Teresa, or you.

A personal reflection about legacy has value in and of itself. With some attention to it, you can define on your terms how and why your life mattered. You will have provided insights for others into some of the qualities they may not have recognized while you were living. The point of a legacy is that it outlives you.

Across a generation, the mosaic of individual legacy statements represents a collective story. Like the release of the soul from the body at life's end, these stories (and more importantly, the energy created by them) can inspire a generational memory that will outlast us.

Chapter 33

Serving the Greater Good

A UNIQUE SET of attributes is brought together in creating a wellness network and Wellness Forum. These include education, life and work experience, perspectives, interests, and personality characteristics. The members can leverage these assets and capabilities in the service of something bigger than if pursued individually. The group's latent energy is more potent than the sum of the parts. For ease of reference, I will call these kinds of collective objectives the *Greater Good*.

Objectives in support or expansion of the Greater Good could relate to the Bigger Picture factors described in Part One. These might include environmental awareness, support, and action, finding antidotes to the darker sides of technological developments, or creating solutions to soften the impact of change on a vast, aging American population. The possibilities are limited only by the interests, imagination, and energy of the members.

I have a specific interest in and commitment to the establishment (or restoration) of enlightened national governance. I will use generational activism in reestablishing the accountability of our elected representatives as an example of a Greater Good initiative.

Imagine setting aside party divisiveness for the good of strengthening the collective power of aging Americans at a time when we most need it. If we put the economic, political, and pure voting power of senior Americans to work, marketers and politicians would have to notice. We have dollars, we have time, and we can get to the polls (including mailboxes) by the millions.

If we are not proactive, our silence will yield further generational disadvantages. Although adults aged 55 and older are the largest potential voting bloc in American history, we have not been able to come together around any cause apart from the aftermath of 9/11. Think of the opportunity for going on offense, if nothing else, as a form of defense of our status quo.

Social Security is a favorite target for federal expense reduction. Remember, though, that Social Security payments are not a gift to us. Social Security is an *earned benefit* rather than an entitlement. The SSA trust funds represent what you paid into the program during your working life.

When your elected representatives are debating this issue, they signal that you may not receive what you contributed. This benefit is more important than ever for the population entitled to receive it. It is worthy of a fight.

Those we have elected to represent us are more likely to listen to the well-funded special interest groups whispering in their ears (far out of the earshot of the constituents who elected them). The American citizens' needs mean little to nothing relative to political policy decisions. Princeton professor Martin Gilens and Northwestern professor Benjamin Page analyzed 1,779 policy issues in detail. They sought to determine the relative influence of economic elites, business-oriented and mass-based interest groups, and average citizens. The unsurprising conclusion was,

"The preferences of the average American appear to have only a minuscule, near-zero, statistically nonsignificant, impact upon public policy."[142]

How is it possible that the voices of voting Americans have no impact on our representatives? There is something deeply wrong with this. In the next chapter, "Radical Seniors Save the Country," I offer a potential cure for this systemic malignancy eating away at the flesh of our republic.

Aging Americans are not now effectively organized to have their voices heard. However, a shift could begin within the structure of wellness networks and Wellness Forums by collectively getting into incumbents' and candidates' faces on issues that matter to us. We can develop the same representation and advocacy that other grassroots special interest influencers have created.

Without regard to gender, race, ethnic origin, religion, education, and political preferences, senior Americans possess enormous potential for reordering political incumbents' priorities. If we can focus on our common challenges rather than our differences, our social and economic needs can be made clear and evident. This unity might have additional beneficial effects on the understanding, relationships, and well-being of those that participate in the effort, crossing the silos that have traditionally separated us.

As much as politicians and the members of younger generations may wish for us to "go gentle into that good night," we cannot. We must make a little trouble on our way out the door. The point is not to take anything from other generations but to use the social, political, and economic muscle we now possess to protect ourselves and leave them better off when their time comes.

---

142. Source: https://scholar.princeton.edu/sites/default/files/mgilens/files/gilens_and_page_2014_-testing_theories_of_american_politics.doc.pdf

Chapter 34

Radical Seniors
Save the Country

"ONE NATION, INDIVISIBLE" has given way to "one nation drowning in debt and hopelessly divided." In many ways, we have become a nation of conformists embracing passivity. Or at least this is the apparent condition as we have elected and re-elected what have turned out to be political representatives lacking the leader part of the skill set.

Many elected officials have done little but use their positions for staying in office as long as possible. They run for re-election and win 90 plus percent of the time.[143] The citizens electing them permit this to occur by not taking their electoral responsibility seriously.

We have blindly elected and trusted presidents, Congressmen, governors, and mayors to do the work of assuring fairness in the use of our tax dollars. Yet we stand by and witness their perpetual tugs-of-war over differences large and small. What levers get pushed and do not depend upon whose votes or financial support matter more to them at the time. Our elected representatives assure that short-term power tactics, special interests, and political slipperiness undercut longer-term efforts. A prime example is the failure to address the looming crisis in Social Security that has awaited attention for decades.

---

143. Source: https://en.wikipedia.org/wiki/Congressional_stagnation_in_the_United_States#Overview

Increasing the feed for an already dysfunctional federal bureaucracy is an exercise in futility. It is ironic that Congress, government departments, and regulators persist in passing laws and invoking rules that call for excruciating accountability from American companies and individuals. *The taxation privilege comes with no concomitant responsibility for the usage of the money collected.* Our tax dollars are viewed as a commodity to be disbursed by them without measuring or reporting return on investment, efficiency, or productivity.

Our elected representatives' unwillingness to adapt our republic's governance to the times is the immovable object. Why would they? Their current management rules, policies, and shadow processes serve their interests, including continuing incumbency.

We occasionally elect well-intentioned people, but they quickly discover a system requiring them to focus on re-election rather than upholding their principles. Even one high-minded person with the best values, intentions, and selflessness will have virtually no impact. This individual has to wait out frustration, the snail's pace of change, and the influence that only comes with years of incumbency.

George Friedman, in *The Next Decade*, writes of an American public that has "...lost both civility and perspective", and politicians "...who cannot lead because they are capable of neither the exercise of power nor the pursuit of moral ends." The process is a free-for-all with no long-term vision for the complex economic challenges we face as a nation. A solution that might require ten years to develop, fund, and implement, has little chance of seeing the light of day. It is no wonder that the system is failing.

Our elected officials' collective efforts will not magically transform into trusted and dependable leadership. Unless there is an active effort to shift their perspectives, their primary goal will be perpetuating their incumbency. They routinely trade away opportunities to serve the

Greater Good. There is no better example than gaslighting our citizens in the course of their (non)response to the challenges of Covid-19.

As mentioned in Part One, our government representatives' unreliability has taken its place as a Bigger Picture factor. There is little accountability to the constituents who granted these representatives dominion over them. And unfortunately, we haven't insisted on it.

The question is, do we remain passive, hoping this dysfunction will self-heal if we ignore it long enough? Or do we take on the reformation of this leadership malaise as a generational imperative? In the context of Chapter 32, "How to Leave a Legacy," restoring accountable national leadership would be a powerful generational legacy.

Shareholders can force out company management for failing to deliver on commitments. Consider American citizen-voters as the shareholders in our republic. We should expect the same kind of accountability from our representatives as is required of the management of any public company. If those elected to manage our nation's affairs fail in their promises and responsibilities to us, we should vote them out at the first opportunity.

American seniors could undertake a collective, committed, long-term effort to replace the people who currently occupy Congressional seats. Over time, we could substitute people who will support their constituents' interests and work with them. This effort could restore the fundamental premise of representative democracy: *service to the people they swear to represent.*

The currently dominant two-party system appears unlikely, for now, to be a casualty of the failure to govern in the best interests of all Americans. But perhaps another party could begin a shift in the matter of accountability to the citizens. Though beyond the scope of this book, I could envision a new *Gray Party* or Peoples Party of Americans 55+

that reflects their collective interests and requirements. Its formation and senior-centric platform would prove that our democracy can "... flex and adapt according to the context and requirements of the times."[144]

Who cares if it takes a new party structure and 20 years of effort? This reformation could begin in the pursuit of the collective purpose and meaning of a Wellness Forum. No matter the form of hyperlocal organization, without a beginning, there can be no transformation.

'We the people' should be carrying on the thoughtful long-term vision of our country's Founders. History, including their own words, tells us that they took their responsibilities very, very seriously. When we prove to incumbents and office-seekers that the 55+ cohorts are activist voters, their hearts and minds may discover ways to support our interests with greater vigor.

My comments do not suggest the projected demise of America as a global power and leader—our country is not going away. We are and will remain a leader in almost every category that counts. However, we must develop and deliver solutions addressing the fundamental requirements for tens of millions of aging Americans and other citizens in need. This crisis is here. It will not get better with time.

Shifting power back to the citizen voters is a three-step process: First, demand clear articulation by any office-seeker of their positions on the issues important to you. Make sure that their key promises are on the record. Video recordings capture the person speaking the words and therefore are the best way to document the candidate's position. Second, continuously confirm whether their statements and actions remain consistent with their public promises. Document and expose any

---

144. Source: This point was eloquently made by Alexis de Tocqueville in *Democracy in America*.

indications of a lessened or abandoned commitment. Third, actively work to vote them out at the first opportunity if they don't live up to their pledges in any material way.

People will spend tens of millions of dollars to get elected to the U.S. Senate. Donors and candidates spend billions of dollars on presidential elections. Why is that monstrous amount of money needed? One overwhelming reason: to garner your attention long enough to get your single vote.

Political races are almost always close. Ten thousand votes (in most cases, many fewer) in virtually all local or state races, and many for national offices, decide the outcome.[145] Until the polls close on any given election day, your vote is virtually priceless.

The only radical thing about enforcing commitments made to citizens is that we have allowed it to slide for so long. We should have insisted upon this simple form of electoral accountability a long time ago. "We, the people, grant the opportunity to serve... and we the people take it away."

We have ignored the enforcement of public record accountability by incumbent politicians to our significant disadvantage. Our nation has been ill-served by our failure to insist upon honor in the promises made by them. It is time to take our part of national responsibility much more seriously.

145. Wikipedia, List of Close Election Results. https://en.wikipedia.org/wiki/List_of_close_election_results

Chapter 35

End-of-Life Exploration

LIFE'S ENDING IS the last item on our bucket lists. But it will come even if you don't write it down anywhere. Most adults seem uninterested or uncomfortable discussing death unless it is about someone else. I cannot imagine a topic for seniors that is worthier of exploration and understanding.

End-of-life readiness is an essential conversation. Seniors more readily view their decreasing lifespans and healthspans as realities. These discussions will help us help each other get to a place of equilibrium in considering our close-to-final moments.

The objective for such end-of-life exploration is to prepare for the moments leading up to our last breaths. It will eventually arise in your awareness. Considering how you might approach the end of your life can be freeing. It might liberate you from fear and anxiety that may otherwise be present.

If we reach the age of 65 or 70 today, our average remaining life expectancy is about 15 years. By age 65, though, you are already a lottery winner: up to 20 percent of your age-group peers will have already passed away. Some died during childbirth, others from accidents, suicide, chronic diseases, rapid onset organ failures, and many other ways.

Others, including you, may live a full lifespan and expire due to so-called natural causes—aging out of living.

Birth and death are two experiences common to all living beings. They are physiological passages that represent the bookends of living. The last moments of life for almost everyone are as predictable as the moments of birth. This knowledge is readily accessible to all, but I suspect the Google search inquiries for "end of life" are many fewer than, "Where is the closest Starbucks?" Here is a link to a short reference guide from the National Institute on Aging, *What Happens When Someone Dies?*[146]

There are two main ways people consider death:

> *Death reflection* is a relatively positive reaction to the fact you will eventually die. It is a process of coming to terms with your eventual death by examining and contemplating your goals. Death reflection engages your rationality. It may stimulate you to answer the questions, "How will I cope with the approaching end of my life?" "How do I want my handling of it to be remembered by those who survive me?"

> *Death anxiety* involves a relatively adverse reaction to the idea that you will eventually die. It can engage a range of emotions, perhaps including fear.[147]

Worrying has little to no value in influencing outcomes—death is no exception. Your resistance is fuel for what you are resisting. You can worry all you want; death is never in doubt.

---

146. Source: https://www.nia.nih.gov/health/what-happens-when-someone-dies
147. Source: "Memento Mori: The Development and Validation of the Death Reflection Scale," *Journal of Organizational Behavior*, November 5, 2018, and https://onlinelibrary.wiley.com/doi/abs/10.1002/job.2339

You can make your consideration of your final moments into a creative process—and why not? Consider envisioning and perhaps even writing a final life-ending scene for yourself. Imagine it is the finale of a movie you are starring in and watching. Creating such a depiction could result in a comfortable and serene placeholder. It could be the method to displace all the other scenarios you might otherwise imagine. Imagine a creepy version of a Grim Reaper movie playing over-and-over in your head.

Whenever negative thoughts of your final days or hours arise, shift them to a situation when you may have said, "If I died here and now, I would be happy." What did you feel, see, and hear? Who was present? This recall is the ultimate power in the now. *A moment once thought by you as perfect could be adopted as your last visualization.*

I have created several scenarios for approaching my death. One is getting comfortable in a bed with freshly washed sheets in a cool, windowless room. In my favorite sleeping position, I listen to some soothing but majestic music played just a bit louder than usual. Beforehand, I arranged for my best friend to turn out the light. Once in the off position, the switch will remain that way forever, and my life is complete.

I envision this as the painless surrender of my earthly presence through sleep. How could you be fearful of something so familiar? It is merely another night of rest. As a scene-placeholder to manage death anxiety, what could be better?

Other visualizations I have created are in nature. In the filtered light of a coastal forest, I rest on a boulder warmed by the sun. I can see the vastness of the ocean from where I sit. As the rock and I become one, the setting's grandeur fills me up. Nothing more is needed.

In another, I lay next to the water on an ocean beach. My eyes are closed, and I feel the sun on my body. As I rest, relax, and listen to the waves, my body warmth slowly merges with that of the sand until there is no difference.

Another way to deflect potential death anxiety is to decide now that you will choose to be the watcher of that moment when it approaches. The watcher is a unique perspective within your soul, enabling spiritual separation from your body. Most of us have had moments of sensation that led us to recall, "It was as though I was looking down at myself," or "I was watching myself move as if in slow motion and saw and felt every detail."

This choice might enable you to say, "I have waited a lifetime to see what this is all about. I am going to take it all in." Doing this will enable you to put away any worry or anxiety you might otherwise harbor and focus on the experience.

Why not choose the best possible observation post for viewing what could be among the most captivating moments of your life? If you do, you can stay curious to your last breath. You can take that unique and exclusive knowledge with you. Think of it as a parting gift to yourself.

The unfolding of your final scene will almost certainly have context and details different than you imagined or visualized. So what? You will have readied yourself for the light going out (or the bright and welcoming lights coming up—as many who have had near-death experiences have reported), whether you live out your placeholder creation or a different one.

Through visualization, you created a comfort zone for your passage. By so doing, you avoided the expenditure of a lot of living time and discomfort resisting in advance, and ultimately in vain. Shaping a vision for the end of your earthly passage is the act of a creator—someone who is free.

Chapter 36

Soaring

—⚡—

BY THE TIME we reach middle age and are on our way to becoming seniors, we more-or-less have what we have, know what we know, and are who we are. Once expansive and flexible beliefs may, over time, have hardened into what we claim as the truth.

We may view the methods we have used to navigate our lives as the only way to manage through the rest of them. We may even want to hang on tighter to the bindings that have kept us in one piece to this point. They are the knowns that have become part of our comfort zones. We may default to the status quo, even if it is now working against us, or may no longer exist.

We continue to rely on the assumptions, perhaps long misplaced, that underlie any essential part of our self-image. When challenged by others, we are quick to defend. We have sharpened our defenses to protect all our flaws from close examination. We are experts in keeping our blinders firmly in place.

It may have become difficult to listen to positions that do not have some alignment with ours. If they do not, we trust that those offering them must be ill-informed or merely unworthy of notice. There is nothing as reassuring as the comfortingly familiar voice heard in our echo chambers.

Likewise, we may continue to have difficulty rationalizing who we might have been with who we are today. You could call the gap between who you became and who you could have been 'unrealized potential.' That term has always created discomfort for me because it applies.

Carlo Strenger, a psychoanalyst, and author of *The Fear of Insignificance: Searching for Meaning in the Twenty-First Century*, wrote, "A realistic relationship to our [essence, our true and fundamental selves] requires that we gradually achieve self-knowledge... parting with cherished fantasies that we have entertained about whom we are or whom we can be..."

There were times in my life when I felt I was operating at optimal capacity, but I know that I left a lot on the table. I accomplished less and served others far short of what I could have done. I would characterize my contributions to the greater good as deficient compared with my ability to do so. I know precisely where and why the lost potential from my life drained away, but I prefer not to closely examine it for the sake of pain avoidance.

If you aspired to do things that you did not, you might feel, as I do, that your unrealized potential has transcended regret to become irretrievable. Regret is the land of "if only," and "I could have, should have," or "I wish I hadn't..." Reminiscing—revisiting your past through subjective recall—can be enjoyable and pleasant, or a reminder of lessons learned. As passing notions, minor regrets are inevitable.

But some regrets can continue to have power over you in the present. These regrets can be especially palpable when the actions taken (or not), or the words said (or unsaid) are incapable of redress. These feelings can be a parasite on your present—sucking time, energy, and emotion. They can sabotage your efforts to unlock the potential that is still accessible to you.

These are some of the views that keep us tethered to the past. If you have accepted circumstances that have held you back from fulfilling your potential or kept you running in place for decades, you can choose to spend your remaining years with a sense of freedom.

Untethered aging is a self-discovery process that empowers releasing the bonds of your past. A journey into untethered aging is buoyed only by that which will allow you to thrive, "unweighted, unburdened, unbound, tied only to that which would lift [you] higher..."[148]

Part of untethered aging is a courageous acknowledgment and release of the past. You can part with any regret, remorse, pain, loss, suffering, and disappointment you may still carry. Untethering is not denial or avoidance of ownership of your life. It is a choice to live a life of psychological freedom.

This letting go process opens the way for embracing a different and more satisfying way of living. It is energizing. You can give full attention to the opportunities for growth through the remainder of your life. You are free to express a greater degree of self-interest without shame or apology.

You can relinquish the feelings of having been a hostage to work, the needs of others, and a myriad of distractions. You can focus on what you can yet create. Realizing more of your potential can now become a fresh and new reason for living. "I am not yet done. I will create with all that I have, know, and am."

What is possible will almost certainly be different than it once might have been. But it can enrich your life and those who you will have the

---

148. The joyful heart is the buoyant heart—empowered to rise above its circumstances, unweighted, unburdened, unbound, tied only to that which would lift it higher, untethered from anything which would pull it down, pull it under or suffocate it. *The Joyful Heart*, Alyssa Underwood 2017

opportunity to serve. You might not be a world changer, but you can be a life-changer for one person or a few. In the words of the venerable sage, Dr. Seuss, "To the world, you may be one person, but to one person, you may be the world."

Most of us do not have the opportunity to impact more than a few people in our lifetimes. If we act purposefully, we can expend our remaining potential in the service of others. We can help others close their fulfillment gaps. You have not yet missed the chance to serve others and, in the process, achieve a greater degree of personal fulfillment than ever before.

The best approach to living in a state of well-being may be viewing the rest of our days as *perpetual*. "I have all the time in the world." By so doing, we can ease our minds of concerns small and large. You may feel a sense of this comfort by reading *The Tree Ripens*, a short poem by Rainer Maria Rilke:

> Do not measure in terms of time: one year or ten years means nothing.
>
> For the artist there is no counting or tallying up; just ripening like the tree that does not force its sap and endures the storms of spring without fearing that summer will not come.
>
> But it will come. It comes...[149]

You can release time constraints by owning the fact that you are the creator of the rest of your life. You need not feel rushed. It is your creation to be revealed on your timeline.

---

149. René Karl Wilhelm Johann Josef Maria Rilke, "Viareggio," *Letters to a Young Poet*, April 23, 1903

Just like the tree in Rilke's poem, season-in, and season-out, we are biological organisms on a trajectory. Perhaps the best of significance is accepting our cycle of living and enjoying it day-by-day—permitting happiness to be our keel, the stabilizing element.

I have offered personal perspectives in *Untethered Aging*. The decade of my sixties was full of life events that made me wonder whether my best years were in the rearview mirror. For a while, I felt sorry for myself and had a difficult time seeing a way forward. I felt stuck, discouraged, and sometimes sad.

Through my reading, research, and conversations with other seniors, I discovered that my feelings about aging were, to a great degree, generational. They reflected the doubts and concerns of other seniors. I began to consider a 'how-to' approach for living my senior years with more curiosity and creativity.

In thinking through the hurdles and possibilities, I began to see that it is not inevitable that our senior years must be ones of decline, disappointment, and decay. We need not spend years on the sidelines until our expiration dates arrive. Self-reliance coupled with collective power —social self-reliance—represents a reliable change platform for seniors.

There can be freshness in your senior years of living. Choosing untethered aging is to release the bonds that had you believing the best you could hope to do in the future is the best you were able to do in the past. No matter the visible condition of the outer wrapper looking back at you in the mirror, the person inside remains vital, vibrant, and hopeful. Open yourself to living your remaining years in freedom. Free in your mind, free to create change, free to serve others, free to be happy, and free to be very much alive.

Appreciation

With gratitude for inspiration and support in the creation and completion of *Untethered Aging*:

Steve Chandler, Russ Verney, Jeff Holtmeier, Alex Cyrell, Tom Liguori, Tom Long, Sookha C., Cheryl Dellasega, Lynn Powell, Natalie, Nico and Arizona Paradis, Branden Scalera, and the memories of all my beloved animal companions now on the other side of the Rainbow Bridge.[150]

---

150. Source: https://www.rainbowsbridge.com/poem.htm

About the Author

William Keiper is an author of nonfiction in the areas of personal and business transformation, aging, and self-help. He is a former NYSE, NASDAQ, and private company CEO, and holds degrees in finance, law, and global management. He is known for his no-nonsense pragmatism and urgent approach to creating rapid change. He is committed to helping aging adults and businesses do things differently as the result of seeing things differently through his writing, speaking, and consulting.

CONTACT THE AUTHOR AT
www.williamkeiper.com

AMAZON AUTHOR PAGE
www.amazon.com/~/e/B0070ZM592

Books by William Keiper

Untethered Aging

Life Expectancy—It's Never Too Late to Change Your Game

The Power of Urgency—Playing to Win with Proactive Urgency

Cyber Crisis—It's Personal Now (also available as an audiobook)

Amazon for President

Apple for President

Walmart for President

Made in the USA
Columbia, SC
25 March 2021